PURPLE HEARTS
AND SILVER STARS

PURPLE HEARTS AND SILVER STARS

Poems, Rants, Essays and Short Stories
Direct from a Trans-Women's Soul

JANICE JOSEPHINE CARNEY

To order additional copies of this book, contact:
Xlibris Corporation
1-888-795-4274
www.Xlibris.com
Orders@Xlibris.com
25586

CONTENTS

Book Three:
The Transition as My Marriage Was Coming to an End

Book Four:
Finding, Me My Life As Janice Josephine Carney

AN AUTOBIOGRAPHY

By
Janice Josephine Carney, BA
(Law Studies, University of Massachusetts),
Executive Director of FORGE
(Florida Gender Equality Project,
a 501(c) (3) non-profit organization)

In 1996 I celebrated a year of sobriety and began a journey of rebirth. That year I developed confidence in myself that previously I never experienced. I took my personal collection of notes, diaries, and tapes from my year in Vietnam and begin to organize them into a book.

In 1997 I completed the manuscript and titled it *One Heart One Mind: one man's memoir of a tour of Vietnam*. The book not only dealt with my year in Vietnam but with the emotional cost of the war on my soul and psyche. With assistance from Jonathan Shay M.D., Ph.D., the author of *Achilles in Vietnam* (a book about combat trauma and the undoing of character), I tried unsuccessfully to get my book published. In 1998 I legally changed my name from John Joseph to Janice Josephine and my writing now included transgender issues. I felt that I had come to terms with my trauma from the Vietnam War, and I was ready to move on.

In 1999-2000 I wrote and performed a play "I Was Always Me." The two-act play is a monologue of my transition from John to Janice. In the fall of 2000 I had my first article published in the *Transgender Tapestry Magazine*.

In 2001 I was the subject of a documentary: "*TransJan*" produced and directed by Katherine Cronin. Its premiere at the Provincetown International Film Festival opened the door for me and after each screening; I conducted a Q&A about transgender issues. The latest screening of "TransJan" was in 2002, when it was selected to be one of the films for the Tampa Gay and Lesbian Film Festival.

In 2001, in Boston, while performing readings of my poems and rants at Slams, I met the writer Toni Amato. Shortly after that meeting I begin attending Toni's creative writing workshops at Women's Words and later attended one of him weekend writer retreats. That year I presented "TransJan" and sat on panels at the Transcending Boundaries Conference at Yale University and at Speak Out, a conference at Bunker Hill Community College in Boston. My most challenging event that year was the L/B/T/Allies Strategy Summit in Vermont, sponsored by the National Organization for Women.

In 2002 I continued to do workshops using creative writing as a means of getting people to open up about transgender issues. I also put together a course of study on transgender issues called "Transsexuals are Human Also." I conducted creative writing workshops at the Midwest L/G/B/T/Allies College Conference. Out of this conference came 'my transgender monologue,' and, as "My Vagina Monologue," I performed this at the St Petersburg Metropolitan Community Churcher's Talent Show, and it was published in the summer issue of the *Transgender Tapestry Magazine*.

This year I have presented creative writing workshops at the International Foundation for Gender Education in Philadelphia, the New Hampshire Transgender Resources for Education and Empowerment at the University of New Hampshire in Durham, and at Silver Threads, a weekend retreat on St Pete Beach.

I have put together a collection of my poems, rants and essays that are directly from a transwoman's heart called "Purple Hearts and Silver Stars." One of my short stories was published as part of Mary Boenke's *Trans Forming Families, real stories about transgender loved ones.*

Later this year two short stories will published in anthologies, *Pinned down by Pronouns (http://www.convictionbooks.com)* and *Transgendering Faith,* Pilgrim Press, 700 Prospect Ave., Cleveland,

Ohio. I am an active member of a local group of women artists called "Women Artist Rising" with whom I share my poems, rants and stories at various WAR events (*http://www.womenartistsrising.com*).

My new column "*Perspectives from a Trans-woman*" that started in a local newsletter is now in syndication.

FOREWORD

This collection is unique. There are many sites on the Internet from which anyone can get an insight into the life stories of transsexuals and other persons that feel compelled or somehow drawn to bending and blending gender or even switching from their gender of rearing. Some sites provide candid reviews of personal life stories filled with recognition of differences and longings to be of the opposite sex. Other sites offer encyclopedic information of trans phenomena or resources, and yet others supply chat rooms for like-minded individuals or the curious to explore, exchange, and question. Books and videos as well as movies have covered much of the same ground.

All these media introduce life stories or vignettes that candidly tell of family, upbringing, and life experiences of growing up wishing to have been born Jack instead of Jill, or Mary instead of Mark. And innumerable media tell of what its like to undergo surgery in an attempt to affect such a change. And then there are many accounts of what it is like to live the desired life after making the desired change. These multitudes of expressions apply to the life and feelings of transsexuals and transgendered individuals of all stripes.

But I know of no other collection of writings that offers the intimacy and insight in how this sort of a life FEELS. Janice, in heart felt and pain blank verse conveys the loneliness of growing up and living with a dark secret that, due to no fault of her own, she has lived. Her plain language strongly describes the bigotry and taunts she experiences and the extents she went through to deny her feelings for the sake of her wife, family and others. One of the most poignant features she repeats is having sacrificed being loved for her gender choice. Her poetry speaks for thousands who

14

JANICE JOSEPHINE CARNEY

lack the voice, desire, or courage to expose such inner pain and finally joy. Her words move any sensitive reader to decry society's prejudices that forced her and others like her to bear such hurting and shame for being sexually different in how they live and how they love.

Although the title of the book refers to war medals very little of it is about war or its awards. The book is a compilation of thoughts and reminisces of feeling like a female and desire to live as a woman. Janice relates that she, as many like her, was willing to risk death in combat to prove herself a MAN particularly in the eyes of others. But her military battles were less daunting then those she felt within her. She finally won her personal war by obtaining the surgery she craved. The emotional price she paid was very high.

In one-way or another the book expresses the cries of thousands of transsexuals and others sexually different. You can't read this volume without being touched.

Dr. Milton (Mickey) Diamond PhD
Director, The Pacific Center for Sex and Society.
University of Hawaii

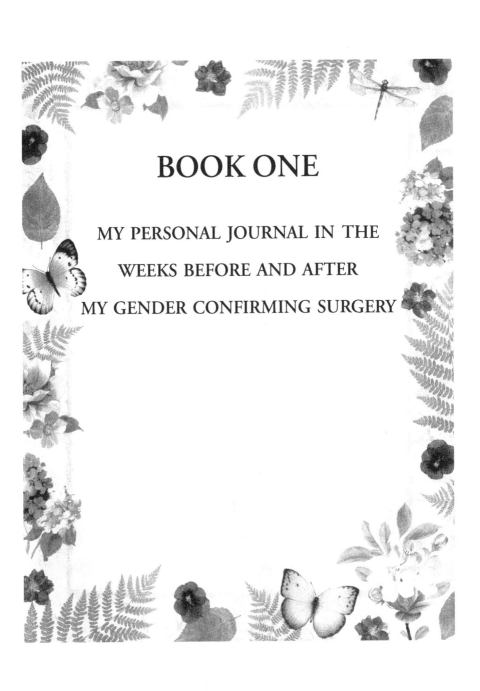

BOOK ONE

MY PERSONAL JOURNAL IN THE WEEKS BEFORE AND AFTER MY GENDER CONFIRMING SURGERY

PURPLE HEARTS AND SILVER STARS

Purple Hearts and Silver Stars
    Are meaningless awards.
Meaningless after arriving home,
    Home from the horrors of war,
To still have emotions in your heart
    After the horrors of war,
To still be able to look up at
    The clear night skies,
To see the stars and still be able to cry,
    That is a meaningful award!
Purple Hearts and Silver Stars,
    Are meaningless awards.
When the horrors of war
    Have left your Soul cold,
When the horrors of war
    Have left you tearless,
Have left you emotionless—
    Tearless and emotionless.
Under the clear night stars

LOVE IS GENDER BLIND!

Love is gender blind.
When I was young, I fell in love
With a boy.
When I was young,
I fell in love with a girl.
When I was young, I was told
That love is color blind!
When I was young, I fell for
A dark skinned boy.
When I was young, I fell
For a light skinned girl.
Love is color blind, I was told!
No one told me that
Love is gender Blind!
OH! Said I, if love is color blind, then
I can fall in love with a dark skinned Boy!
No! They said, Love is not gender blind.
Love is colorblind!
But! Said I, with the wisdom of a child,
Love is gender blind, also and I kissed a boy
Years passed. Love has come and gone
My gender has changed,
Still I know Love is both gender and colorblind.

A PERSONAL JOURNAL

My journal from the last weeks before my surgery:

[Jan 31. 01]

I am doing my monthly budget. I live on my monthly Vietnam Disability check. My bills, mostly a loan, and credit cards [money for my surgery] eat up most of my income. That's fine, Tess [my cat and companion] and I will do fine.

All I want is to feel whole, to feel like a human being. I want to belong to mother earth, not be a freak of nature, Living on the edge of a lonely planet. My spirits are high. Tomorrow I take my first step of the surgery process, I stop taking my hormones. I am fearful of the return of dark facial hair and being called Sir and Mister! I just die a little inside, whenever I get that Mister, with the "you freak" stare!

[Feb. 1, 01]

I had lunch with my dear friend Christine today. I am so grateful for all she is doing, knowing I have a friend taking this journey to Trinidad with me.

I was on the Internet last night, and stumbled into a message of hate from the revered of the Westborough Baptist Church. Rev. Phelps's message of hate! "God hates fags. Com" the message said: "Trinidad Is a grotesque malignant tumor in America's bowels. Dr. Biber is mutilating God's creation, to satisfy perverted lust!"

I do not understand how one man can be so full of hate, in the name of God! The God of my belief makes no mistakes. The Reverend Phelps, Dr. Biber, and I all were born for a purpose. I was born with the spirit of a woman in the body of a man. Dr. Biber was gifted with a passion and a skill to help two spirited people. The Rev. Phelps was born with a calling to preach hate! Our circle of life comes to a meeting in a small mining town in Colorado.

My God made me in his image and spirit. With or without a penis, I still am in the Goddess image. I am wise enough to separate the fools from the Sages. Only a fool will make a statement like "God hates fags." Only a true Sage would dedicate a part of his life, to helping a misunderstood minority of the population.

When I was young and full of fear and shame, Reverend Phelp's message would have pushed me off that bridge. My soul cries for today's children who are jumping of bridges after reading "God hates fags."

[Feb. 2, 01]

I am listening to Billie Holiday: "in my solitude, I am praying dear Lord Send back my love." In my solitude I sit in my chair. Filled with despair. With gloom everywhere. I am so mad in my solitude. I am praying, dear Lord please send back my love."

I love Billie Holiday; as painful as my life has been I cannot feel half the pain she lived through! I just live with my own pain, my own discrimination; I stay away from so many places where "my kind" are not welcomed! My love, after a 25-year relationship is long gone, and no amount of praying is going to bring her back!

"Sunday is gloomy, my hours of slumber, will never wake the new. Not to where the black night has taken you. Gloomy Sunday. In the shadows, my heart and I have decided to end it all. Let them not grieve. Send my way cards and prays. Let them all know I am glad to go. Death is no dream for in death I am caressing you with the last breath of my soul. I will be blessing you gloomy Sunday gloomy Sunday, dreaming, I was only dreaming No, my Sundays are not gloomy any more. I go to a wonderful church in the morning. On Sunday night I return to the church for an AA meeting. Billie never did overcome her addictions, sadly.

[Feb. 3,01]

Memories are overwhelming me. At last night's woman's meeting, I talked about my long marriage. My long-time therapist called it a toxic relationship. Other women were talking about controlling spouses. I, at last, am coming to terms with the truth that was overshadowed by blind love! For 25 years, my wife convinced me that I was too nervous to drive a car! Too stupid to know when to get a haircut! Too feminine in the way I dressed! I drive a car today, I have long flowing hair today; I am no longer too masculine in the way I dress! I am not nervous, I am not stupid, I am not dressing to please someone else, and today I look at a happy reflection of myself before I go out the door. Why do I miss my ex-wife so much, why do I cry so often? In time I will find my true soul mate, a person who loves me for the transsexual that God made me.

[Feb.4, 01]

I am lost in a past that never happened. The closer I get to my surgery, the sadder I get. Saddened my lack of a past as a little girl.

On Feb 25th I will wake up in a hospital bed. I will be 51, and celebrating my first birthday as a woman! All my memories are those of a man, a boy. A twilight zone of a lifetime of brain washing! I have won the gender war! Now can I overcome the battle scars?

[Feb.5, 01]

My brother, Dave, would have been 53 today. I miss him so much.

He always knew about my gender confusion, yet he never told anyone. I wish he were here, today to see I have found peace. I know he would be happy for me!

[Feb.6, 01]

I was born in 1950; Christine Jorgensen was reborn in 1952. Jan Morris was reborn in 1972. I will be reborn in 01. An empty brain sometimes is a good thing. I am in a complete peaceful contentment. I have recently read Ms. Jorgensen's and Ms. Morris biographies. I have found that the three of us have a lot in common.

Our sense of loneliness from early childhood. A sadness that haunted us into our adulthood! The medical compassion we found in Dr. Benjamin. They found their doctors to heal their pain. I have found mine Dr. Biber, in a small mining town, Trinidad, Colorado. One thing has not changed since the fifties; we are still hated and feared! We are hated by so many and loved by so few. All three of us have lived a life overwhelmed by the fear!

> Fear of ourselves, fear of taking that leap into womanhood,
> Fear of spending the rest of our lives alone.
> Fear of rape
> Fear of violence, just for living.
> Fear of using a public restroom.
> Fear of the way we walk
> Fear of the way we talk
> Fear of just living a 24-hour day!
> Fear of being rejected by our family, friends and even our churches.
> It seems our lives are condemned to solitude!

Feb. 7, 01

I just got back from spending some time with my two daughters.

Every time I think all is right with my babies, the pain returns. I feel so useless. I cannot be a father or a mother to them! I try to be a loving parent. I do hope some day they understand my situation, and accept me for who I am. I could not save my marriage. I cannot go back to pretending to be a man. My children do not want me to meet their teachers. I am so lost, my tears are like the great falls, I am so lost on what to do. I cherish the time I spend with my girls, yet I hate the loneness and pain that I am in when I leave them.

[Feb.8, 01]

I am finally committing a successful suicide! I am killing John Joseph Carney. I am killing my mother's favorite son. I am killing my baby sister's hero. I am killing Tom and Tim's big brother. I am killing my children's father. Is the act of having gender reassignment surgery, not killing the man?

My heart is crying; my soul is smiling! How can I be so sad, yet so glad?

I fear my relationship with my children is disintegrating. In a failed marriage, it is the children who get hurt the most. The parent who still sleeps in their house is the hero. The parent who leaves is the villain. Throw in a transsexual father: that makes it my entire fault. This is not the place to try to justify an ugly divorce. All I can say is my wife had another man's baby before we were even divorced. Still I came out as the "bad guy/bad girl!" I was always me. I always was too feminine! Through the course of our 25-year marriage, my wife changed, not me. Now I am free, now I can change. I pray that following my heart will not cost me the love of my children. I know it has cost me the love of my baby brother and sister; they killed me off two years ago!

Should I surrender to society, should I surrender to the norm?

Should I do that, should I kill off Janice Josephine? I know now if I try to do that, in the long run, I would be killing both John and Janice. My two spirits can live together. We can live a happy sober life in a woman's body! In a man's body, in a man's world, the depression, the booze, the drugs will kill me.

[Feb. 9, 01]

"One Day My Soul Just Opened UP" is the title of a great book by Iyanla Vanzant. Three years ago I had that same epiphany. My soul opened up and screamed: I cannot live like this any more!! So started my journey from a world of lies and deceit, alcoholism, and overwhelming depression. I overcame it all by forming a strong spiritual base. I know I am not alone in believing that God,

Goddess, is a divine spirit that is in all of us. I can gain strength in knowing I am following my inner divine spirit. In living the life of a woman, I am not a freak of nature. I am part of nature. I am being true to Mother Earth. I am following my divine spirit. I am fulfilling a plan for me that was destined by a higher power. I am a living faith in a higher power. I am a divine spirit. I am alive for a divine reason. I was born with two spirits as a gift. I thank Mother Earth, and Father Sky.

Feb. 11, 01:

I recently read a crude quote from a columnist, named, Jonah Goldberg that for some strange reason is paid by the National Review.

The quote concerned transgender activist Riki Wilchins:" She has a giant scar on her throat from were they took a couple of inches off her Adam's apple. Presumably she's got a worse scar elsewhere."

I am having Surgery elsewhere in five days, and I have been extremely reflective as of late. I am blessed with a small Adams apple, so I will not have that scar. To Mr. Goldberg the point is, for a woman, having a penis is a scar. Unless, Mr. Goldberg prefers penises on his sex partners, I would think he gets it! I, myself am happy to have the scar removed!

Scars are part of all of us. I am sure, Mr. Goldberg has a few. Some scars are physical; some are emotional. No one sees my deepest scars. No one can see Riki's deepest scars as well. I have emotional scars. Scars: that never will heal. Deep wounds from a 25-year marriage that came to an end! I have even deeper scars from my year in Vietnam. These too are emotional wounds that never will go away! Black spots in my brain and soul, from a war, I still am trying to understand. Scars on my soul, for all us Vietnam Veterans! I have a black hole in my soul from all the years of gender confusion.

I also have physical scars that, ASSHOLES, like Mr. Goldberg can see.

A scar on my right leg! AS a young transsexual; I played alone in a fantasy world. Jumping of a roof, chasing tinker bell, I cut my flesh on a nail. When I was a little older, my brother cut me with a knife. A small scar, between my eyes. When I pencil my eyebrows: I cannot miss the small scar. My last year in high school, I heard the scream "hey fag". I have a small scar under my lip from that punch in my face!

When I put my lipstick on, I cannot miss that little scar. When I paint the nails on my right hand, I cannot miss the little horseshoe shaped scar. That little scar came from a small piece of flying hot steel. A little, reminder, of Vietnam. A reminder of how hard I tried to be a man! I know Mr. Goldberg, and Riki will never read this. I am not even sure why I wrote it! I think I wrote it just to say, no one should, make a joke out of anyone's scars.

Feb. 13,01:

I am a transsexual, I always was a transsexual, and I always will be a transsexual. I am not sure if that makes me sad or glad! I will have a Vagina as of Feb. 22, 01. My life as a functioning woman will begin. So many people will still call me sir. So many people will still call me a freak. It is so sad! Yet I am so glad that I know I am a woman.

[Feb.14, 01]

Valentines day! Big deal. Maybe next year I might have a change of heart. Maybe next year I might be walking arm in arm with a Valentine. After my surgery, I would like to do a little mainstreaming. I would love to go dancing in a straight club without fear of my life! I wonder if I ever will have that comfort zone. Will I ever be able to just dance in peace? I am grateful for the gay clubs for supplying a safe place to dance. I am tired of dancing alone. No gay man has ever asked me to dance. No lesbian has ever asked me to dance a second time! Maybe I never will have a dancing partner. I will not know without trying. I no longer will be a woman with a penis but I still may never have that dance floor to shine in! It seems the world just does not get it. I will just be another woman with a natural desire to dance and shine in the light of the night!!

[Feb.15, 01]

The spirit of the journey is real. I am a gifted person blessed with the spirits of both genders. I am made up of a penis and a vagina, a flat hairy chest and full blooming breasts, these are just body parts. My soul is that of both a man and woman.

I prefer to have the body parts of a woman; I am more in touch with Mother Earth as a woman. I know that a part of my spirit is and always will be that of a male. My soul, that part of my spirit that is all woman, will celebrate, on Feb 25th.! I will be a 51-year-old man in a young woman's body.

On my birthday I will begin making new memories. I will have a new life. I pray to all I believe in that I have the strength to be open and proud of who I am. I will not let the hate and fear make me deny who I am. There is so much pressure in our society to be a man or a woman-cross that line and finger pointing begins. Fear will not force me to deny my two spirits.

I was strong enough to let the woman in me free when I had a penis. When it is gone. I must have the strength to explore my life, as a woman to it's fullest!!

[Feb. 16,01]

I watched a tape of Dr. Biber speaking at a seminar in 1991. I am confident that I have picked the best doctor available to perform my surgery. Any question about Dr. Biber's age is of no concern to me. I am delighted to have a doctor who is older then me!

[Feb. 17,01:]

I am off to clean St. David's Church for the last time. I have been an active member of St. David's for fifteen years. The church sexton, for ten years. It is the church where my son received his First Holy Communion, and Confirmation. My two daughters were baptized, as well as receiving their First Communion there also. I served as a member of the Church's Vestry. I served as Jr. Warden. I served on the search committee that hired their current minister. All those years of faith and devotion, yet all I hear is silence, as I leave for my surgery!! As I locked the door for the last time, I could almost hear the sigh of relief From Mother Diane and her congregation. Thank God the freak is gone! As I was leaving, I took a copy of Sunday's bulletin.

On the eve of leaving for major surgery. On the eve of my fifty-first birthday. There was no request for prayers for me. On the list of birthdays there was no Janice Josephine Carney! It was like I never existed!

[Feb.18.01]

Some where in the realm between reality and fantasy Peter Pan exists! With her fairy friend, Tinkerbell. Some times I think I live in that realm, that separate dimension that includes Fairies, Leprechauns, and Gnomes. We all dance together in this dance called life. Peter Pan is a girl. As a child, I often got into fights defending that fact. I always lost the fights, yet I know Mary Martin was Peter Pan. Robin Williams tried but he was not Peter Pan. The magic of the Peter Pan story is the genderless of Peter Pan. The world of Fairies, and evil pirates. In Peter Pan's realm, among the fairies, gender is not an issue. Peter Pan has the best qualities of men and women!

Sadly, I live in a realm where it is a major sin to blur that gender line. Men are strong, aggressive and domineering. Women are sensitive, nourishing, and weak. To weaken is to emasculate! At birth, a doctor looks at our genitals and DECLARES! It's a boy! Or it's a girl! From that point on, our lives are defined. I am not Peter Pan; I am more like Tinker Bell. A small light in a huge dark world. In my dark world, we people with that mixture of the genders are left to find our shadows without any help. I live in a society that is holding my shadow hostage! In my realm there are no evil pirates pushing us off planks. In my reality there are evil Christians, just plain evil God fearing citizens feeding my kind to the crocodiles!

[Feb. 19.01]

My last night before leaving for my surgery and my mind is a maze of rapidly moving images. My past, present, and future are all here at the same time! My cross-dressing past! A lifetime of purging with to many trips to the good will box. Telling myself: "I will never wear woman's clothes again." Today I live as the woman I always knew I was. My last visit to a goodwill box was to purge myself of men's clothes. >From that liberating day three years ago, today I am on my way to correct that birth defect.

A walk in the sun in a soft flowing sundress. Those baby steps lead me to the big leap I am about to take. Today is my last day of pain and confusion! Oh! I know the pain will always be with me. At last, though, I am doing what is best for my spiritual, physical, and mental well being. I am a woman. I know that and Dr. Biber knows that. Soon I will be able to sit down and pee in a public bathroom without fear of being arrested! That init self is worth $13,000 and a little physical pain!

[Feb. 19,01]

It's 9:55 a.m. and I am strapped in and ready for take off! In 2hr. and 30 min. I will be in Colorado Springs. From there it is about a three-hour drive to Trinidad. All those years of pain and confusion: how can I stop this insane obsession to dress and act like a woman? My Inner Spirit is glowing and my soul is smiling. I may be a little different from the accepted norm but I am not insane. The decision to have radical gender change surgery is a deeply personal decision. I am not being pretentious when I say I have been dreaming about this day since I was around ten years old! The day is coming when the rest of the world will perceive me as I have always seen myself.

I am not fooling myself. I am a mixture of both genders. I always have been and I always will be. I know today that I am not cursed. I AM BLESSED! My gender war is over. I am no longer fighting who I am!

We are getting the safety speech. I wonder if we have to have an orderly emergency exit, should I exit last? Children and women first, then the men, and last but not least transsexuals!

I have to rest my racing mind. Dr. Biber, here I come.

More thoughts While in the sky on Feb. 20,01:

I am reading from a collection of meditations as I fly over the clouds. I do wonder if I ever will find a safe place to live! Is there such a place for me?

I can close my eyes and envision my haven. I can hear the sounds of the ocean crashing in. I can hear the ocean birds chirping. I can feel the sand between my toes. I can smell the salt air. Can I find this peaceful place, a piece of earth to grow old in? The reflection, of a full moon, on a quiet beach. A sky, full of stars, a warm night. Maybe even a gentle soul to hold my hand. My faith will lead me to this place.

I am half way to Trinidad and to excited too take a nap. Am I having second thoughts? I would be a fool not to have some doubts. Am I being selfish in having this surgery in spite of hurting so many people? Do I have the right to put my children through this? Their father becoming a woman. Is stopping my pain worth the pain I see in my mother's eyes? Is my having a peaceful spirit worth losing the love of my brother and baby sister? It is all so stupid. Why does my happiness hurt so many people? I have spent my whole life being what other people wanted me to be. I cannot live like that any more.

Doubts, do I have doubts? No! I have no doubts. I am on the eve of my fifty first-birthday. I have not had a day of true serenity in my life. I am a woman. All I want is the freedom to express my femininity without ridicule. I know my children love and accept me. I deserve to have that measure of peace and serenity, as I grow old. My smile and glow will brighten someone's day. Yes! After all these years I have no doubts. I deserve to be whole: one body, one mind, one spirit. Every inch a woman!

[Thoughts on my arrival in Trinidad on the night of Feb. 20, 01]

Wow! What a day! Trinidad is a sight to behold from the town's highest point. A small ex-mining town on the old Santa Fe Trail. It is amazing. Transgender souls from all over the world come here to heal their wounds. Here in this obscure little town in the Southwest corner of Colorado. In a true sense I will be reborn in a few short days!

Feb. 21, 01

I woke up at 1:00 a.m. and could not get back to sleep. Henry Kissinger was on the TV for a split second last night. I relived the early seventies. Not even gender reassignment surgery can erase my memories of Vietnam. It is 3:00 a.m. and I am dressed for my 9:30 a.m. appointment with Dr. Biber. An interview with the doctor and a physical, then I will be on my way to the hospital. For a change my tears are not of sadness, they are tears of joy! I think I am feeling grief. Sadness for a lifetime wasted trying to be the man I never could be. A sense of loss for never having the experience of being a girl. In a moment of solitude I remember my last bout with depression, my last drink, my last suicide attempt. This space is too small to list all the wonderful people and organizations that opened the door I am walking through today!

Still Feb. 21, 01

It is 3:00 p.m. and I am in my room at San Rafael Hospital. The emotions I felt during Dr. Biber's qualifying were immense. Reliving a lifetime of confusion and shame. At long last a doctor that said, "I can fix it." I have set up my altar on the window still. As I stare in the flame of my candle, I wonder if a life of loneliness is the price I will pay for finding inner peace. I never felt so scared and happy at the same time; so alone yet not alone.

The reality is hitting me I am actually having my penis inverted! That birth defect is being corrected! No! John Joseph is not dying; Janice Josephine is not being born. This doctor is correcting a mistake a doctor made on Feb. 25, 1950. It's a boy! Wrong it's a girl! RIGHT! Every attempt I made at confirming my manhood is flashing by me.

My attempts at sports in high school, joining the Army, serving in Vietnam. Working at a hardhat job. My long, lonely marriage. I could go on and on! A couple of hours ago, I was standing naked in front of Dr Biber. Stark naked, tears running down my eyes So many miles from home. In this old building in this old mining town. Looking into the eyes of this gentle man with a big smile. No problem here! I can fix this! For the fist time in my life a doctor that can fix me.

I am standing in front of my altar that I have set up on my hospital room's windowsill. Gazing into the candles flame, I pray:

I praise a loving God, I praise a loving goddess, I praise Mother earth, I praise Father Sky! I give thanks for all the spirit guides that are here with me. I give thanks for tomorrow; I start my journey as a physically correct Woman. Tomorrow my spirit, my soul, my physical body will be united as one.

It's 10:00p.m; I am waiting for medication to ensure a good night's sleep. 6:00a.m. will come quick; 6:00 a.m. is surgery time!

[Feb. 22, 01]

It is 5:30a.m, where is Dr. Biber? I am ready. I have decided to have the surgery! OF COURSE! In one hour I will be completing my metamorphosis! As corny as it sounds, my childhood dream, of weaving a cocoon and busting out a beautiful woman is today a reality.

[Feb. 23, 01]

I am in pain and discomfort. I look and feel horrible. I am at a loss to describe how great I feel! That thing, between my legs, that thing that controlled so much of my life, IS GONE!

[Feb. 24, 01]

I am in too much of a fog to collect a single thought! I am in a fair amount of pain. Every thing just happened so quickly. I woke up back in my room. Dr. Biber assured me that he completed another beautiful piece of work. I am just so tired and weak. I have to sleep.

I am at peace!

Feb. 25,01

I just had my first birthday cake as a woman. I am in possession of a legal document that declares; I AM A WOMAN! Looking in the mirror at the foot of my bed, I look awful! My hormones are all out of whack. My nights are a combination of hot flashes and the chills. Every few hours I have to change my bloody pads. It is impossible to find a comfortable position. There are people in the trans community who oppose gender reassignment surgery. They call it maiming our bodies. As I lie here in pain, and looking as bad as I feel I say to them No! I did not maim my body. I lived fifty years with a maimed body. If the price of correcting my body is a few months of pain and discomfit, that is a small price.

No more tucking and hiding that smelly penis between my legs!

The money issue is still scary. My bank account is under ten dollars. I have a loan and charge cards to pay off. It is going to be a battle to get my health insurance to reimburse me. Is it possible to put a price tag on peace and serenity? I think not! Yet, that is what I am paying for! I say to all my transgendered sisters who have found peace and serenity without surgery, bless you. We must stand tall together and fight for our civil rights. We have to show the world that we are proud of who we are.

Feb. 26, 01

Some thoughts, after reading Thich Nhat Hanh's essay "Going Home:"

"God is not a person but not less than a person. If you are to penetrate deeply into reality, you have to get rid of notions. We can speak of the wave as high or low, beautiful or less beautiful; Coming or going, being born or dying."

For so many years I thought of myself as less than a person. I wasted my life away, agonizing over notions of how a man should act. In one of these depressing states, the God that is in my spirit spoke to me! I was ready, that cold winters day, to die in the waves of the Atlantic Ocean. Every time I purged my self of my female identity a piece of me died. Today I understand why my inner Goddess called me away from those waves of death.

I am a female today. In a sense I was reborn. Then again I was always a woman. Is God a person? I do not know. I do know I am not less than. I am a person!

Oh! I just received another beautiful spring arrangement! Flowers and cards! I know now I do have a family, not blood related: More importantly, love related.

In his essay Thich Nhat Hanh went on to say" The capacity for loving God depends on your capacity for loving humankind and other species." At times I feel like another species! If human beings can not get along with each other how can they ever get along with my SPECIES? I was just dozing off, when I heard voices out side my door. Oh! They do that kind of surgery here! I wonder what kind of surgery they were talking about.

A short while later I was watching the TV news. A minister was discussing the new federal program to fund church programs. He was quite upset. His point of contention, federal funds going to programs at the Unitarian Universalist. "The UU is not a church of faith and should not receive federal funding." WOW! What a viewpoint! After eighteen years as a devoted member of a Christian church, I was showed the door when I crossed that gender line. In my UU Church in Manchester, NH, I am just another human being worthy of love and respect. Every day I have been in the hospital, I have received cards from my friends at my new spiritual home.

All I can do is laugh; all I can do is live my life as I see fit. "The capacity for loving God depends on your capacity for loving humankind and other species." So says the Buddhist monk Thich Nhat Hanh.

Feb. 27, 01

"If you practice looking deeply inward you will see that the notion of birth and death can be transcended." [Thich Nhat Hanh]

How did I ever get the strength to be me? The basic twelve steps from the Big Book of AA lead to my rebirth. Before I could work on my outer body I had to work on my inner spirit. I had to cleanse my body of alcohol and drugs. Looking inward I transcend birth and death. Being reborn is a term tossed around by a lot of Christians. Yet they do not have a clue what it means. Looking inward, finding ones self, is being reborn! I was reborn in 1996, when I took step one, and admitted my life had become unmanageable due to my drinking. It took two years, before I had an emotional rebirth. In 1998 my spirit was set free. I purged myself of all my men's clothes. I changed my name to Janice Josephine. That is being reborn! We have to remember I was always me. Today as, I lie in my hospital bed, recovering from my surgery I can now say not only have I been spiritually reborn, I have been physically reborn.

There is no real birth or rebirth, there is no real female or male. There is only that continuation of the spirit. The spirit that I am, that I always was. That I always will be. Living or dead that spirit will continue on in some realm!

Feb. 28, 01

I am out of bed, dizzy and feeling weak. My face and body is a wreck. I have been off my hormones too long. Friday I will be back on my hormones. Friday I will start my journey home. I am out of thoughts. I am out of words. Standing nude in front of a mirror I see my new body for the first time. I AM A WOMAN! A tired middle-aged woman. I just want to go home and LIVE!

April 5, 2001:

I am home, I am healthy, I am ecstatically happy, I am ALIVE. I have many new challenges to face; I know it will not be easy. Why did I choose this path? Look at my life and you will see, it was meant to be.

Way back in my youth I would spend my nights in my sisters nightgowns, hiding my penis between my legs. I would cry myself to sleep with dreams of the beautiful woman I would be some day. There were failed attempts at sports. There were failed attempts at making friends. My favorite place in the whole world was the library, my favorite books Madelyn, and the tales of the little girls in the tiny orphanage in Paris. I spent three years in the fourth grade, one in a Catholic School, two in Boston Public Schools. I was, John Joseph, I was a boy! No one had a clue what was wrong with john! I stuttered, I would cry for no reason. I had no interest in my teachers or any of the other kids. After school I would disappear into my own world; hiding in a closet in my sisters' clothes. The humiliation of being caught by my father, by my brother, led to fear of who I was. Going in to Jr. High I purged myself of my secret collection of women's attire. This was the first of many trips to the good will box!

Going into the seventh grade, I was confident, I hardly stuttered, I had glasses so I could read, I was wearing" boys" underwear. My favorite movie was the "West Side Story" I would walk around singing "I feel pretty". As the Beatle's were taking over the airwaves, I was singing "People" and day dreaming about the beautiful gowns Barbara wore. Nobody knew why John was so different. No one knew why john just wanted to be alone. Well, I had another stash of women's clothes! During this time I met the only girl I would date through high school.

In 1966, I started high school. I had a girlfriend. I had two male friends one that I had desires for that I could not understand. A week before school started I had purged myself, yes, another trip to a good will box. I would keep my love for Barbara S. and Judy G. a secret. I made my mind up "I was normal" I was going to fit in. I became a Beatles fan, a Rolling Stones fan. The four years went by in a blur. It was not long before I was hiding women's attire. I kept my true desires a dark secret. I dated my dear girlfriend and took her to the prom. 1969 came quick. I graduated from high school, still clueless about what was wrong with John.

In September of 1969 I made an attempt to talk to my father about my problems.

I was 19 years old, listed as 1 A for the draft. I already had a small scar under my lip from being gay bashed. I still was fighting my preference for women's clothes. My grandmother was telling me to visit her sister in Nova Scotia. My "girlfriend" had no interest in getting married. (Years later, I would find out she found the real woman of her dreams.) I did not get too much out before my father gave me the "No son of mine speech". The next day I joined the Army and requested duty in Vietnam. The main pattern in my life, continued. Out of shame and guilt, I did what I did not want to do! Out of shame and guilt I purged my self of my female wardrobe. To prove to my father, to prove to myself, I guess! I joined the Army to prove I was a man. This space is too small to discuss my three years in The U.S. Army. I survived a tour of Vietnam. And a year and a half in Germany. It is obvious the Army did not make a man out of me!

In 1972 I received my honorable discharge from the Army and returned to my hometown. It was not long before I had my own apartment and a super wardrobe. I was a 22-year-old kid with his/her first taste of freedom. I quickly got out of control. Drugs, alcohol, sex for money. What was wrong with John? I still did not have a clue. In 1975, I took another trip to the good will box. I swore never again. 'I am a man". I have to deal with it. By 1978 I married a girl eight years younger then me. I took a hardhat job. I was a married macho, hard drinking Vietnam Veteran. I was a living-breathing lie! For over twenty years, and three wonderful children, I lived that lie. With a job at the Post Office and lots of alcohol. With many trips to the good will box, with pain, shame and guilt, I lived that lie. I was a man!

By 1996, the PTSD, had caused me to take a disability retirement from the US Postal Service. That year after dressing up, drinking, taking a lot of prescription medications I laid down to die. The next day I woke up in a hospital bed very much alive. I woke up at last!

I asked myself what is wrong with me?. After an extended stay in a VA hospital, I started attending AA meetings. In 1998, with two years of sobriety, my sponsor and I had a talk. Why was I still so depressed? Why did I still have thoughts of suicide? Why was I so close to another drink? The same old question, what is wrong with John? My marriage fell apart. I was living alone, with a new wardrobe. The shame and guilt was driving me back to the bottle. For the first time in my life I opened up to another human being. With a river of tears and a shaking body. I opened up. I am not a man, I never have been a man, and I never will be a man! That got his attention, yet without scorn, he gave me the best advice I have ever received.

"Do a fourth step inventory, take a honest hard look at yourself, and look inward." That I did! My last Trip to a good will box was to purge myself of my mans wardrobe. I lived as women, for a year out side of Boston. I got support from the International Foundation for Gander Education in Waltham Mass. I joined a gender support group. I Legally CHANGED MY NAME TO Janice Josephine. In my second year I started hormone treatment and I contacted Dr, Biber in Colorado.

I attended a couple of transgender conferences. I at last found out what was wrong with me! My earliest initiation was right, the whole world was wrong! I am a woman, I always was me! With or without surgery. With or without hormones. I was born with the soul and spirit of a woman.

BOOK TWO

WORK FROM MY

CREATIVE WRITING WORKSHOPS

THIS COLLECTION OF WRITINGS IS DEDICATED
TO MY DEAR FRIEND: TONI AMATO

All of the work in this section came from Toni's creative writings workshops.** Opening phases such as if they was a museum of me what would it contain. I picked up a picture of a potato and had to write about it. A hand full of shaving cream, go with it.

THANK YOU TONI FROM THE CENTER OF MY GENDER QUEER SOUL! WITHOUT YOUR CREATIVE WRITING WORKSHOPS, I NEVER WOULD Have had the self esteem to write "Purple Hearts and Silver Stars."

**   for information on Toni Amato's workshops call Toni at (617) 491-2938 or email *TTONIAMATO@AOL.COM>*

IF THERE WAS
A MUSEUM OF ME

(What would it contain?)

A museum of me! What a concept. What is a museum? Fine art, science, the children's museum, museums of history. A museum of me, WOW! Me! Born Feb. 25 1950 in Cambridge Mass.

Declared a boy by the medical profession. There would be a picture in the museum, of me with a penis.

YES! The raw me. I am really out of it, on writing on this one. A museum of me. How would my school years be represented? My adolescent years for all to see.

It would be a room called loneliness. A place of emptiness, to sit on the floor and ponder.

O K, let us move on to the East Wing. A portrait of Jean and John at the Senior Prom. A moment to treasure.

On to the West Wing. This wing would be dedicated to my war year. Complete with a day one picture of me in Vietnam, and a 365-day in Vietnam picture. The whole world could see the incredible aging solder.

OH! Here would be my good conduct medal. You see, I find it comical that they hand out good conduct medals.

Give it some thought! What is bad conduct during a war? On to the north wing. Here would be my drag pictures! Oh! I know there still are some old pictures still floating around in some TS magazine somewhere.

Some one I am sure could even dig up my old Phoenix ad, {*massage by petite TS, oral entertainment extra.*} Beware of DRUGS, ALCOHOL, SHAME, GUILT, PROSITITUTION, DEPESSION, SUICIDE TENDICES, And ALL THE HIGH LIGHTS OF THE NORTH WING.

I DIDN'T ASK YOU TO STAY

I DIDN'T ASK YOU TO STAY, I DID NOT ASK YOU TO STAY. No one asked me to stay the day I moved out. It just was a matter of necessity. My son asked me, how could you stay? How can you watch your wife stay out all night? Even my daughters did not ask me to stay when I told them I was moving. They did not ask me to stay so I left.

My mind is racing as I am informing people that I am leaving again. This time I am leaving New England. Yes, I am leaving New England. A lot of people are asking me to stay. It is a nice feeling, it serves a need. That human need to feel wanted.

I am going far south, near the Gulf of Mexico beaches. Two miles from a VA Hospital. A short walk to the moll. A moll with two, possibly three, coffee shops. Seminole, Seminole, the Seminole wind is calling me home. The hot hazy days, the warm comfortable nights. No one is really, really asking me to stay. No one is holding me tight, and whispering in my ear. Squeezing me so tight that it hurts and whispering in my ear" Please, please do not leave."

In a mixed way my children are happy to see me go; our loving but strained relationship needs distance. They know my heart has been in Florida for years. They have been with me in Seminole; they have seen me basking in the Florida sun. They have seen that smile, that the sights, smells and sounds of the ocean brings to me. My ex wife said," I love you" to me the other day! Wow, what a shock that was!. "Be careful, it is different down there. I love you and would not want anything bad happen to you." No! She did not ask me to stay; She did not hug me and whisper in my ear, "Please do not go." She knows my passion for the ocean.

She knows my passion for sunny warm days. My passion for long warm nights. Fear! What does she fear? Terrine Summers, on the eve of my move, another name is added to our wall of remembrance.** Terrine summers; A Lt. Commander retired from 22 years in the navy. Guilty of being an out and proud transwoman in Jacksonville, Florida. The penalty for being a transwoman in Jacksonville a bullet in the back of the head.

I did not ask you to stay, where can I go from that?

I wanted Terraine to stay

I wanted all the transpeople who are now names on a wall of remembrance to stay. I wanted them to stay here on Mother Earth until it was their time to go from natural causes.

I want to go when it is my time to go. When the Goddess of my faith ordains that it is time for me to go. No, not when a misguided fool with a gun, no not short dead in Vietnam or in Boston or in Florida. No, not shot in the head by some asshole! No, not at the hands of some angry man that never even knew me. No, No, when it is my time to go it will come, but that moment will not be deprived me. No not by the hand of some deranged angry man.

"I love you" my ex wife said to me the other night, Even a transwoman, can be loved, someone still loves me.

** *http://www.gender.org/remember*

Gwen Smith's wall of Remembrance website

Dedicated to the memory of murdered Transgender souls

"QUACKS" (This was written as a mindless exercise Quack, Quack, Quack take that sound and let you pen race across paper for fifteen minutes. My delightful fair-minded editor, pointed out that it was extremely critical of doctors, and that I was confusing TV Doctors with reality. I decided to edit it and to keep it in my book but with a sort of explanation of where my mind was when I wrote it. I was struggling to find doctors that were experienced with transgender medicine. I also was dealing with Heath Maintenance Organizations that refused to cover the medical services that I needed. The anger boiling inside of me was at the Insurance companies, not the doctors and lawyers. It is the HMO's and big health Insurance companies that have taken the medical profession and turned it into a heartless medical industry. Over the last several years I have come to realize that transgender medicine is new and rear for most doctors; Yet, I have found wonderful Doctors that have treated me and guided me through my surgery and post care.)

QUACKS

At the height of the bubonic plague in Europe during the 1340's, charlatans took advantage of people by selling useless salves and acuminating treatments. These were the original Quack's, they where not Doctors!

WOW! Not much has changed from the 1340's to the 1900's. The aids plague that hit North America provided another means for quacks to make money of the sick and dying. Once again charlatans were selling useless selves and accumulating treatments. It is inspiring to know that creative quacks are still alive and well! Sadly, low-life's that feed off other people's misery have always been around and still are today. The modern day Quacks are chief executive officers of pharmaceutical companies and health maintenance organizations. One thing that has changed from the 1340's is the medical advances of twentieth century science.

The other day someone asked me, "What ever happened to Susan Pewter, the diet guru of the "Lets quit the insanity" books and video tapes. Well that Quack! Was marketing the cure for alcoholism. A combination of vitamins and exercise, and you will never drink again. She and her commercials were pulled off the air!

Quacks! The whole medical Industry is made up of quacks! That is the medical Industry. When I was young it was the medical profession, now it is the medical industry. We used to have medical heroes like Dr. Kildare, Ben Casey, and Dr. Marcus Welby, MD. The Hippocratic oath was alive and breathing back then. Today hospitals are supposed to make profits; if not, they are shut down. If sick people cannot afford to pay for treatment, show them the door. After all, this is a profit making industry; it is not just a hospital any more. This take over of the medical profession by accountants and ceo's of Health Insurance companies has tarnished the good work off all doctors. You do not see doctors portrayed as heroes on weekly TV shows any more.

Quack! Quacks Quacks, I tell you they are all Quacks! Last year, I had a—life saving surgery in Trinidad Co, by Dr. Biber. The medical name for the surgery is "INTERSEX SURGERY." The Quacks at the top of the Veterans Administration and at Blue Cross call it "Gender alteration surgery." They say it is an elective surgery, as in a non-essential Cosmetic Surgery!

Quacks, Quacks, Quacks, I tell you they are all Quacks!

Dr. Biber calls it correcting a cognitive birth defect. The Quacks call it useless and wasteful.

Dr. Shay, my Doctor at the Veterans Administration Hospital told me three years ago that the surgery would be good for me. He said that it might help heal a lifetime of pain. The Quacks said no. "All you need are more anti depressants, more anti anxiety medicines. "You will be fine."

Quacks, Quacks, Quacks, I tell you they are all Quacks! There is only one other profession with as many quacks. You know, the one that Shakespeare felt so strongly about! Lawyers!

Now, I have to deal with Quack lawyers

To sue the quacks running the medical industry.

Quacks, Quacks, Quacks, I tell you they are all Quacks!

THE POTATO

Simply a potato! Maybe, maybe not. I was raised on potatoes; potato pancakes, mashed potatoes, potatoes covered with tomato sauce, sliced hotdogs and green pepper, fried with potatoes. It seemed every meal had some form of potato.

As of late I have been re-thinking an old saying of my fathers: "Sometimes you have to play Mickie the Dunce." I never gave that expression much thought. My father and I were far from close. He seldom talked to me but often ridiculed my dress and way of walking.

But, I regress from the potato. It was on a recent excursion to Boston that I studied the Irish potato famine statue. This bronze statue of a hollow cheeked mother and her hungry children is an awesome tribute to all those that died during the Irish famine. The mass exit of the Irish from their homeland, immigrating to America's big cities, was the direct result of the potato. Or, I guess from the lack of the potato.

So I got to grow up in the greater Boston area, instead of in a quiet Irish village. Yes I am here today due to the potato. Mickie the Dunce comes back to me now. The intense hatred the Irish immigrants received in Boston, as they sought jobs, haunts me today. I relate to it now. My great grandfather was ridiculed and called dumb Mick on these streets. On these same Boston streets, I have been ridiculed and called fag, sissy, Queer, fruit! Blood has dripped down my chin after being physically attacked on these streets. Harassed because of my long hair, my style of dress, the way my hips swayed when I walked.

I blame it all on the potato! Yes it all was due to eating too many potatoes as a child! Maybe I am wrong; who knows. Yet today, I walk these streets proud of who I am. Just glad to have this time to be the real me. Praise the potato! Praise the potato! Its lack of rooting led to me finding my true gender roots here in America.

THE GREEN SUBMARINE

I did it. I shaped and molded it; yes, I created it.
Here it is "TA DAUGH"—The green submarine.
Oh, I know, once long ago, there was a yellow submarine.
But do not be confused; this is the green submarine:
More powerful—more more! Well just plain more than the yellow
    submarine. It is fantasy time. My eyes are closed.
My body has gone numb. I am tiny, tiny, tiny enough
To fit in to my green submarine! Up periscope ;our mission:
To eradicate the northeast of all bigots.
As we head up the mighty Charles River, I meet with my crew to
Define our mission. The question is asked: What color are bigots?
The answers fly out. Black, White, Brown, Yellow, Red!
They come in all colors
As the choppy river pushes us North, our meeting goes on.
What do bigots look like? Once again the answers fly out.
They are short, they are tall, they are fat, they are skinny.
Oh, This is getting complicated.
How can we eradicate the northeast of big bad bigots, if we do not
    even know what they look like?
What if they look and act just like us? My crew is immersed in a
    food fight.
Our mission is in shambles. They look to me for inspiration.
I look up to my picture of the Pope, the biggest and most notorious
    bigot of them all. I pray for guidance.
I touch my Buddha that I carried home from Vietnam. I sense an
    epiphany!

The bigot is in all of us! Our mission can be completed. We all
    must look inward; Yes,
All we can do is eradicate our own bigotries. We do that and we
    have won!!!
Down periscope. Down to the bottom of the Charles River we go.

To quote Monty and Boston's famous rock group, the Barbarians:
"I love that dirty water. Boston, you're my home."

A THREE-PERSON PERSPECTIVE ON "MY LAST DRINK."

A speaker at an AA meeting:

All of the people that I have heard speak at these meetings have come to the conclusion that they are alcoholics.

I have heard many tales of many last drinks. This is one such story; of course the storyteller will remain anonymous

The story unfolds: It was a cold winters day, so I was told, it was the last weekend in January. The middle-aged man who told the story relived it in detail. His wife and children had gone away for a skiing weekend. He was alone for a weekend to be his true self, and to do some household chores. He blinked his eyes and stuttered as he told his story. He recalled starting the day with a shot of Jack Daniels in his coffee and ending the night in an emergency ward near death.

My daughter's perspective of my last drink:

I remember the day my father had his last drink, and the sad day he almost died. My older sister, my brother, and mother were going away for a weekend skiing trip. My father had not been drinking for about two months, this time. He had promised to be good just before we left. It was a raw January morning, when I asked my father, one last time to come with us. I still recall him reinsuring me that he would be all right. He said it would be best if he stayed home to do some household chores that needed to be done.

I do not remember why we decided to go home Saturday night in stand of sun Morning the house was dark and quit when we got home. I went right to my fathers room were he was lying down. We quickly realized something was wrong and called 911.

Now, my story, of my last drink:

It was a raw winters morning back on January 28, 1995. I had convinced my family that it would be best that I did not go on a weekend ski trip with them. I was, in part, sincere about doing some needed household chores. I enjoy doing my household cleaning well in a comfortable dress. I had no attention of drinking. Yet, before I got dressed up I had a shot of Jack Daniels in my coffee. Like any good alcoholic I had a stash of my favorite form of alcohol. I thought I could be my true self, with out guilt or shame, I was wrong. One drink could not be the end of the world, could it? The rest of the Saturday was awash in alcohol and housework, a day of highs and lows. I recall steering into a mirror and crying.

I recall taking a lot of my lithium, Prozac, trazodone, then topping it off with a bottle of beer. Laying down in my favorite nightgown. I dozed off with dreams of Tom Jones. I sort of recall hearing a distant voice screaming DAD! Wake up Dad!! I sort of, remember being rushed by ambulance to the hospital.

It is five and a half years later, and I am proud to say my name is Janice Josephine I am an alcohol and I am proud to say that today I am a somber and free transgender woman.

EMPTY POCKETS

All these things we can carry around in our pockets. My pockets are usely empty these days. Now I carry a pocket book, as in a purse. I find it so much more useful then carrying a wallet in my back pocket. I used to carry a wallet in my back pocket. I had an indentation on my right cheek for years. Now a day my side pockets as well as my back pockets are empty.

I think it all is a gender thing. As a man bulging pockets never bothered me. Now when I am wearing that perfect fitting pair of jeans. I want my thighs and hips to look shapely! Even putting my hands in my pocket when I am walking is a no no. I have to stand tall and walk proud, upright, and straight.

My old self, that poor lost soul, would stroll through life, hunched over hands in his pockets afraid to make eye contact with any one! What do people keep in their pocket? That was the question that started this piece of writing. I was at a somewhat sense of loss on the subject at first.

I remember an incident that happened not to far from here years ago. I was caring a half point of southern comfort in my back pocket. I was on my way to the local hang out, and had plans on spiking my cokes. It was a raw winters day and the sidewalks were iced up and I was somewhat already tanked up! Right there on Springfield street was the woops! A half pint of southern comfort in my back pocket as I went down, Woops!

I felt no pain at first, just wet. I did not even realize the liquored was not just whiskey but also blood. I made it to the mans room at jimmies sandwich shop. I was more upset with having no whiskey to put in my coke then upset over the pieces of glass in my butt! I washed up my self the best that I could, then I went out to face my friends and have a night of ridicule.

The point here is simple! Do not ever put a half pint of whiskey in your back pocket! Icy conditions or not it is not a good thing to do. Oh! Well I am here!

LET ME ADD! I recommend a good AA meeting to all of you that are in the habit of carrying a half pint of whiskey around with them in there pockets!

FUCKIAN SHAVING CREAM!

Lemon flavored shaving cream! AH! AH! I have a hand full of Lemon flavored shaving cream.

OK, I can deal with this. Facial hair-thick black/gray facial hair! I never could afford laser or electrolysis, my only option was shaving real close and real often. That odor is triggering something, like the sudden sound of a firecracker triggers my PTSD from Vietnam.

I feel a similar trigger in that odor that fear of a four o'clock shadow. Facial hairs shooting, out overpowering the heaviest cover-up that money can buy. Of all the things I had to tolerate through my transition, facial hair was among the worst. Well! There was one worse thing, but we will not go there!

This cream in my head, this odor, this smell, this sensation in my hand, this fear. Who am I? What am I?

I am a transwoman! As good as any woman! Why this fear of facial hair? The pressure from our culture is so strong that I deny my very own existence. I have facial hair, I have to run and hide!

The whole world is laughing at me. I remember walking through Copley Square, three years ago. It was shortly after starting my transition, before I begin my hormone treatment. A man screamed out for the whole world to hear, "Hey! That's a man in a dress!" My first instinct was to run and hide. No! Not any more! I gently walked on to the Back Bay train station and went into the women's room. Staring into the mirror, all, I could see was that dark shadow of facial hair.

My anxiety was overwhelming! I was starting to hyperventilate! Women coming and going were staring at me.

I am just a man in a dress! No I am Not! I am a woman in a woman's room where I belong. I was now in the mist of a full-blown anxiety attack. It is time to wrap up this short piece on what it is like being me.

The point is that I over came my fears that day. I walked out of that women's room strong and proud. I took my train home. I cried and I cried some more! I cried a lot that year but I survived. Hormones! hormones! Thank the Goddess for hormones! I still have to shave occasionally but certainly not three times a day!

And most certainly not with men's lemon-scented shaving cream!

SWEET JACK DANIEL'S

Jan.28th, 2002, will start my sixth year without sweet Jack Daniels.

That nip of Jack is not real; at least from here it is not real.

The smell of sweet Jack Daniels is not in the air.

Oh! How I know that smell. "Oh that smell" Leonard Skynard;

'Oh that smell that smell of death."

SWEET JACK DANIELS, SWEET JACK DANIELS

Do you know how close I came to drinking myself to death?

DAMN CLOSE! Six years ago!

Way back, way back, back when I had a penis.

Back when I did not believe in anything.

Sweet Jack Daniels, sweet Jack Daniels,

Fuck that shit!

Last Friday night as I was working on my computer, I received an E-mail:

SWEET JACK DANIELS, SWEET JACK DANIELS.

I was so close, close to giving up.

One drink, just one drink to pull myself together.

24 hours at a time, Sober for the moment.

Let go and let God, friend of Bill. 12 steps to freedom.

Wow! Just the sight of a nip of Jacks Daniels.

SWEET JACK DANIELS, SWEET JACK DANIELS

Do you know how close I came to drinking myself to death? Sweet
    Jack Daniels, Maple walnut ice cream over a warm apples table
    talk pie; now that's sweet. Living for the day Dr. Biber would
    perform his vaginopasty technique.

Now that was sweet. Feb. 24, 2002.

I will be celebrating the first, anniversary of my intersex surgery.

I will be celebrating my first birthday as a full human spirit.

SWEET JACK DANIELS. SWEET JACK DANIELS

Female chemicals running through my soul, brain, and whole body.

My breasts still blooming, my hormones raging
All of me united, united at last. All of me body, spirit soul united
    as one . . . .
Do you know how close I came to drinking myself to death?
SWEET JACK DANIELS, fuck you! I got the last laugh.
I will be sitting on the beach sipping my virgin margaritas.
Hoping to lose my lesbian virginity to a butch along the way.
I lost my heterosexual Virginity to a man in P town; we will not go
    there now!
SWEET JACK DANIELS, fuck you!
Do you know how close I came to missing out on life?
Do you know the power Jack Daniels had over me?
Agh! I am preaching. Oh! Jack Daniels is great.
Great for people that who can handle it.
I believe they are called social drinkers.
SWEET JACK DANIELS, fuck you, for I was not a social drinker.
I drank for all the wrong reasons.
Sweet, sweet life, for all its ups and downs.
Sweet, sweet life, the sun on my face.
Crabs racing across the beach; big goofy birds flying overhead.
Close your eyes; just listen to the ocean.
The sounds, the smells; these are the sensations of life.
Middle aged ladies in two-piece suits.
I wonder hay many lesbians there are on Seminole?
Do you know how close I came to drinking myself to death?

THOUGHTS ON A POEM

{written after hearing AIR AND LIGHT AND TIME AND SPACE BY Charles Bukowski}

Is time and space real? What is time and space?

Ann Frank wrote in a tiny attic, hiding from the Nazis. Could she have possibly written a more profound piece of work, in a three-bedroom condo in Hawaii?

What sparks our creativity? Is it comfort, discomfort, happiness, sadness? Maybe, the places I have been. The space I have walked in. Some good, some bad. These have all inspired me in some way. I have had lapses in my writing: These were times in my life when material goals controlled me. I had let the desires for material possessions conquer my appetite to swallow sunsets, and then reproduce them in words.

In happiness and in pain, I have used pen and paper to try to make sense of the senseless. Could I do better if I left my basement apartment and relocated my widows 2001 or whatever windows it is that I have?

If I sat my ass down in front of a picture window with the most majestic view of the Atlantic Ocean: Would I some how not have the same life time experiences that drive me? The same pains and scars that haunt me; maybe haunt is too strong a word. No! My past does not haunt me; it allows me to see a brighter future.

I sat early this morning with Tess on my lap as my grandfather clock chimed out the hour. I could hear two doves cooing on the grass in front on my window. Tess leaped from my lap to the widow still. The doves continued cooing and eating away. That moment in my basement apartment was living!

My cat, the doves, and me sharing a quiet moment. This is time and space. Could I have had that same moment in a big house? Sure! But would I be more creative in writing about it with a new super 2001 windows soft ware? No!

Creativity comes from within.

always
alone

Why Try To Remember
what I have spenT
A Life Time
Trying To Forget ?

We were asked to draw pictures of childhood memories then write about them:

School is an isolated place. I fear Men! I hate my brother! Why! Why! Why! The only times I am happy are when I am alone and dressed in my sister's dresses, wearing lipstick.

FEAR! What is wrong with me? The girls will not let me play with them. The boys throw rocks at me and call me a sissy. I still hate my brother!

School still is an isolated and lonely place. I still fear men! I went to summer camp once. It was an isolated and lonely place. I fear men. I wet to bed and cried at night. Every one had friends but me. I remember a councilor that had a gunshot wound in his back, from the Korean War. He was the only person who spent any time with me.

The bus dropped us back in front of the old boy's club on Bunker Hill in Charlestown. I remember all the other kid being greeted home by there parents. I finally picked up my suitcase and walked home. School got a little better as I learned to act like a boy.

I never under stood what I did wrong!

Dark bedrooms are scary! Especially when older brothers come in at nighttime and hurt your bum. I was made to promise not to tell anyone!

My big brother just had a triple by-pass. Every one in my family is mad at me because I would not visit him in the hospital. I am not going to go to his funeral!

It should not be so painful to be a child!

THE KID I MOST DISLIKED IN GRADE FOUR

How absurd! The one kid I most disliked in the fourth grade. In what fourth grade?. The one I spent at the Bunker Hill grammar School, the one at the Warren, the Harvard or the last one at St Frances catholic school? Memories are wonderful things; still I am fifty years old. Actually I will be 52 in 75 days.

The kid I disliked the most in the fourth grade. I liked very one, sadly most kids did not like me. I longed for that thing, called" friend'. The point being no one liked me. I was this skinny odd kid. That bought mayonnaise sandwiches for lunch every day. To me I was abnormal, my family was abnormal. To me all the other kids were normal and were from normal families. I was different, with dark secrets that I could not share.

Is my memory capable of going back that far? Capable of remembering any kid from those school years? Some where around the years 1959/1960 I lived on Main Street in Charlestown Mass. I lived on the third floor of a triple Decker. My view from the front widow was eyeball to the elevated train. Out my back window was the huge hood milk bottle on top of the Hood plant on Rutherford Avenue. It was at this house, well playing in my imaginary world that I discovered Peter Pan's secret. Peter was Mary, yes! The boy was a girl. Peter Pan was Mary Martin. It would be many years before I discovered that I was not Peter Pan, that I was indeed Mary Martin. I had lived a life as a woman playing a role of a man.

Memories; back in the fourth grade. Back in that house on main street. Back to that hidden world in the tall grass in the rotary at Sullivan square. I do remember some friend's exploring our sexuality in that tall grass.

Innocence was torn from me that year, we moved to a house on Russell Street. The night visits began. I was in a new school and still in the fourth grade now in the warren school off High street on the other side of Bunker Hill.

I never even got to dislike any one at the Bunker Hill school. Now I was in a new school with a chance to meet new kids to dislike. At the end of that school year I was sent home with a report card, which recommended my repeating the fourth grade.

I was alone, just alone with my fears, with my shames. We moved that summer into a two family house in an old Boston alley near City Square. I re-started the fourth grade at the Harvard School. By this time my Brother was making more nighttime visits to my bed. He was teaching me about sex. He was teaching me about family secrets. He was teaching me about shame and guilt. I had problems with anal bleeding. Problems with bowl movements. My stuttering was getting worse. I could not read well, I had to hold a book close to my face to focus. I feared that the teacher and other kids knew my secret. In the middle of that school year, we moved again. We now lived in a house near Sullivan Square. Across from the sticky and poor spice company

I still was alone with my fears and shames. I was back to the same old teacher at the Bunker Hill school. I finished that school year sitting in the back of the class. I was sent home with a note! "Peter Pan" is a little slow, next year we will try "special" Classes". The words whispered were Son and retarded. I am not sure what hurt more!

That summer we moved to a house on Caldwell Street on the edge of the Somerville border near Sullivan Square. All summer I feared going back to the Bunker Hill school. My mother fearing her strange little child was retarded went to the Catholic Church for help. I was now in a catholic fourth grade. I was a student at St. Frances on the top of Bunker Hill. This was the red brink building that was built after the anti Irish riots of the 1800's. I was in a white shirt, blue pants and blue tie. The poor kid that was not paying for the privilege of a good catholic education. I was still Peter Pan, I still stuttered, I still was with out glasses. The cathocishim now was teaching me that I was a deviate and a sinner. My family secrets were my burden. Who do I dislike from this year? All of them! I remember one day trying to run home. Some of the boys from my class dragged me into the wooded area behind the MDC Pool, and pulled my pants down. They took turns fucking me. My secret was some how knowned by every one. I was, I was, I never did know what I was.

I do not know what kid in the fourth grade I disliked the most. I never got to know any kid well enough to like or dislike.

BOOK THREE

THE TRANSITION AS MY MARRIAGE

WAS COMING TO AN END

ALL MY WIFE'S FRIENDS

Well, I am on the subject of loneliness. the question comes up; what happened to all my friends? When I was married, and had the house in NH with the pool, I always had friends. I have come to the sad realization that all the friendships that were bonded during my long marriage were my wife's; none of them were mine. In the last eighteen months not one of them has called to inquire on my health.

My wife desired to end our marriage, and with the support of her friends, she dived right in to a relationship with another man. I moved out of my home, although I continued to pay the mortgage. I left the woman I had loved for the last twenty-five years; I left my loving children. I moved into a small apartment outside of Boston. I left a nervous wreck, and in the middle of a serous weight loss. None, as in zero, of my life long-friends called! Not one phone call of concern. Who were these people I called friends for the last twenty odd years?

I thought Elaine was a dear friend; we had a relationship that spanned a quarter of a century. Early in our relationship, it seemed as though she actually had a close bond to me than to my wife. In the last year or so I have called her engaging in some long conversations. She made it extremely clear that she would do anything to insure that her friend {that would be my ex wife] got every thing she wanted How does one judge friendship? Sure, Elaine picked up the phone when it rang and talked to me. Yet she never called me out of sincere concern. I guess that answers my question.

All most as long as we knew Elaine we knew Karen. We met at a support group for first time parents; Her son and my son grew up together. When we moved up to New Hampshire, she was a regular houseguest. We even shared our vacation in the White

Mountains with her and her children. On Veterans Day she would call just to say hi to me. All those years I thought she was my friend, as well as my wife's. Karen also has not called me in the last year and a half. She has not even called me on Veterans Day! Not one call to inquire on my well being.

When my wife decided that we were going to home school our two daughters, we met Candy, and she become a close family friend. Candy and I had huge political differences; still, we debated them as friends. Sandy also knew how hard my wife's decision to end the marriage hurt me. I never got one "how are you doing "phone call from her. I have to say the silence hurts. Linda was another long time friend from the early days of our marriage; like Elaine, I considered her to be a friend. I also called her a number of times during those emotional days as the loneness was overwhelming me. She, too, never called me, out of the bond of friendship, I guess all of these friends developed a bond to my ex wife, stronger then any bond of friendship towards me.

I am trying here to understand how, over a twenty-five year period of time; my wife made life-long friends while all I made were casual acquiescences. I was just there, someone to be polite to: I wonder now if my discomfort with my-self was the key factor of this situation. Did the inner turmoil I was living with build such a wall around me that I could not relate to man or woman? For years I thought these women and their husbands were my friends. Zero phone calls leads to zero friends, as I see it. I not only lost my life long-partner, I also lost a lifetime of friendships.

I have learned that as a woman, as a whole person, I am capable of making friends. As a shell of a man with no real inner spirit, I was incapable of bonding with anyone. As a complete spiritual woman, as a whole human being, I am sure a new partner will come into my life, real friendships will blossom.

There is one friend of my ex wife that I left out, my baby sister. She was the one who introduced me Jan all those years ago. She was and still is my Jan's best friend. Naturally, I called her often over those lonely emotional times. She, more then anyone else, knew how devastated I was. I have cried through the phone lines, sharing my darkest fears to her. We discussed some of the remarks the woman I loved half my life had made:

"Get out of my life, I have outgrown you."

"I have wanted to leave you for the last eighteen years. I just was never strong enough to."

"I just married you to make Eddie jealous."

"My woman's group gives me strength, they are my new family."

"You are to feminine I went to be with a real man."

A lot of what I said to my little sister ended up in my ex wife's ears. As sad as it sounds I always called my sister, as she never called me out of concern. Yes her calls added up to zero also! So I just add my baby sister to the list of my wife's friends. I am a complete woman now. I am comfortable enough in my own skin to bond and to make friendships. Today I have completeness in me along with a spirit that allows me to build friendships. I realize now that as a man I never had that. Today I am strong enough to make my own friends, I do not need to hang on to my ex wife's friends, Good by Elaine, Sandy, Linda, and to my dear sister Debbie; you are and always were my wife's friends. I know that you were never friends of mine; I thank the Goddess for all the wonderful true friends that she has brought into my life.

DID I CREATE LONELENSES: FROM, "I WAS ALWAYS ME"

TUESDAY MAY 30TH 2PM, 2000

MY 25-YEAR RELATIOSHP WITH JAN IS OVER. BY ORDER OF THE COURT OF NEW HAMPSHIRE.

I AM NOW LEGAL A SINGLE INDIVUAL. NOT ONLY AM I PHYSICALY ALONE. I AM LEGALY ALONE.

SINGLE, AFTER 25 YEARS, I AM SINGLE I AM 50 YEARS OLD AND SINGLE.

I AM ALONE IN MY NEW APARTMENT. ALONE WHEN I SAY GOODNIGHT

I WAKE UP ALONE AND SAY GOOD MORNING TO MY SELF.

FOR THE LAST TWO YEARS I HAVE LIVED ALONE, IT IS A ODD FEELING

HARD TO GET USED TO. CAN A PERSON LIVE ALONE AND NOT BE LONELY?

IT IS A QUESTION I AM STRUGGLING WITH.

I HAVE COME TO THE REALIZATION THAT ALL THE FRIENDS, I THOUGHT I MADE IN THE LAST 25 YEARS, WERE MY WIFE;S FRIENDS.

THEY WERE JUST POLITE TO ME.

I AM WORKING ON THE SKILL OF MAKING FRIENDS. I AM TRYING TO LEARN WHAT IS A RELATIONSHIP. WHAT IS IT THAT MAKES THAT SPECIAL RELATIONSHIP BETWEEN PEOPLE?

I HAVE LEARNED THEIR ARE TOXIC RELATIONSHIPS, AND THERE ARE TRUE LOVING RELATIONSHIPS. WE ALL HAVE SOUL MATES AND KINDRID SPIRITS.

THERE ARE PEOPLE THE TRULY LOVE EACH OTHER FOR ALL THERE LIVES.

TIME PATIANCE AND HEALING, FINDING MY TRUE SELF, THESE ARE THE KEYS, IN FINDING MY SOUL MATE,

THE KEY TO OPENING THE DOOR FOR A LOVING RELATIONSHIP IS FIRST LEARNING TO LIKE MY SELF. THAT IS THE KEY TO END THE LONLENESS.

TIME IS NEVER ENDING

HEALING A HEART TURNED INSIDE OUT CAN IT REALLY HAPPEN?

IS LIVING ONE DAY AT A TIME REALLY A POSSABILITY.

FINDING MY SELF, HEALING ALL THOSE OPEN WOUNDS. AT LONG LAST I HAVE DONE THAT BUT AT WHAT PRICE?

I NOW HAVE INNER PEACE. HAVING A WALK IN THE SUN, MY HAIR LONG AND FLOWING IN THE WIND,

A DAY JUST WALKING DOWN TOWN AND HAVING A CUP OF COFFEE, WEARING A SEXY DRESS WITH THE RIGHT ACCESERIES.

IT IS A MIRICLE OF LIFE! A FEW THANK YOU MAM"S, JUST ONE SMILE A DAY FROM A STRANGER

ALL OF THESE ARE SMALL ESCAPES FROM MY LONELENESS.

I HAVE FOUND MY TRUE GENDER; I HAVE FOUND THE GENDER THE GODDESS HAD MENT ME TO BE.

IN THE GLOW OF A SUNNY DAY I HAVE NEVER BEEN CLOSER TO MOTHER EARTH, I HAVE NEVER BEEN COSER TO FATHER SKY, I AM TRULY PART OF NATURE.

AT NIGHT TIME I AM ALONE AGAIN IN MY APARTMENT, AT NIGHT I QUESTION MY SELF.

IS LONELENESS THE PRICE I MUST PAY FOR MY GENDER FREEDOM?

HAS RELEASING MY INNER SPIRIT TOSSED ME INTO A LIFE TIME OF LONELINNESS?

SOME NIGHTS I CRY AND CRY! IT IS AS IF I CREATED LONELENESS!

DOOMED TO LONELENESS

It does seem that I am doomed to eternal loneliness. I have a mother, who stopped calling me. She used to call me often just to say that she loved me. The last time I visited, with a shocked look on her face, she exclaimed, "Please do not come here dressed like that." I told her I was extremely comfortable in these clothes. "But I have to live here; what will my neighbors think?" I kissed her good by with a feeling in my heart that I would never see her again

I have made up my mind. I have stopped committing emotional suicide. I cannot go on being my mother's vision of who I should be. My wife, after a twenty-five year relationship, blessed with three beautiful children, told me that "You are too feminine; I want to be with a real man. I what to know what it is like to have sex with a real man." I moved out, leaving the suits, sweaters, pants, and ugly plaid shirts; my wife always said that I looked good in plaid shirts. It seemed every Christmas every birthday I received beautifully wrapped plaid shirts and manly sweaters. Today I dress for the vision I have of who I am. I have released my soul from behind those drab shirts and sweaters.

I was on the subway in Boston very early during my transition from masculine to feminine, and a fellow passenger passed me a note as she exited the train. It said: You are beautiful; you make the world larger for all of us, thank you.

Wonderful words of encouragement from a compete stranger. I wished they had come from my mother. I framed that little note, and I keep it as a prized possession. At a time when most people made me feel like a complete freak, here was a kind soul who just saw me.

Today I dress in long, flower-covered skirts, bright colored blouses, and matching pumps. My wife's leaving me behind, allowed me to move forward. Even in this new loneness, I am more alive then I have ever been. In a suit and tie, I was stiff and awkward on a dance room floor. Today I am alive and flowing when I am dancing. I love the colorful lights bouncing off me. I feel the music through my veins as it controls my body movements. When I am dancing I am alive, I am a woman!

I called my youngest brother the other day. As usual all I got was his answering machine, and as usual he never returned my call. He never calls me back. The last time Tim called me all he did was scream! "Stay away from Ma dressed like that, for Christ's sake! Are you trying to give her a heart attack?" FUCK HIM! The last time I saw him was at my sister's house. I was well dressed, and looked damn good. He looked at me with utter disgust and just blew past me into the other room.

I have a baby sister who used to adore me. Every time I call her now her husband answers the phone and says she is not home. She never calls back, either. At times I feel that they will never talk to me again. This hurts deeply, yet I still love both of them.

I have never been this comfortable in my own skin, at any time in my life. I am on my first month of hormone treatment. I am living for the day that I can throw my silicon breasts away. At times with out breasts, I feel like nothing more than a man in a dress. I am still alone, unsure of who I am, and unsure of which gender denies my existence the most.

I stopped at my older sister's house the other night; I thought she accepted me for who I was. She opened the door with a shocked look on her face. "Oh my God, the kids are here!" The thought of my niece and nephew seeing me in a dress struck panic in her. I myself had no problem with them seeing me as the person that I am. Who should see me for the woman that I am? Should I be forced to an isolated island where no member of my family will ever have to see me again? Isolated from a world that I seem to be offending!

In a moment of weakness, my shame returned. I lied and told my sister's grandchildren that I was dressed up for a play. I left my sisters house in tears. Who will accept me for the human being that I am? I cannot go back to those years of shame and guilt! I cannot go back. I cannot and I will not deny my very existence.

My sister called me the next day and acted as if nothing even happened. She invited me to a birthday party for my younger sister's daughter, who will be twenty years old: she is not a child. My sister said: "Please come as John, mother and Tim will be there. I hung up and pulled the knife out of my heart.

"Please wear normal clothes." Such a simple request, isn't it? I am amazed that my family prefers John that unhappy, alcoholic, overweight, nervous, awkward person. They want him back. Janice is happy, Janice is sober, and drug free. I look good, I feel good, I am not a nervous wreak any more. I am Janice, Why do they want John back?

I am so lonely, there is nothing more I would like to do than spend a Friday night with my family; still, I will decline the offer. I will spend Friday night alone, in a crowd of strangers. I will dance; I will be free of guilt and shame. I will dance alone. Most people in the club are polite and nice. The gay men smile, and say hi, how are you tonight? The lesbians smile and tell me I look good tonight. I will not hear a gentle voice asking me to dance.

I will dance alone. I will flow across the floor like a butterfly. I will be free like a butterfly; like a butterfly, I will fly alone. I will feel the music flowing though me; I will feel the music touch me. I will not feel a warm human embrace as I dance. This overwhelming sense of loneliness has been with me since my childhood. I have always been unsure of what my gender I was. I was unsure of who to play with. I was unsure of what toys to play with. Unsure of what clothes to wear.

On any given night ;I can fall in lust with a man or a woman. Sadly, I have also found out that I do not bring out any desires in either gender. I dance alone, floating like a butterfly across the dance room floor, until the midnight hour. The night owls take over the dance floor then. Woman embracing woman, man with man, woman and man, all moving to the beat of the music. No one asks the freak in the dress, do you want to dance? One lonely transgendered soul alone in the crowd, dancing alone. Some nights

I lose my calm, peaceful feeling, and I let the loneliness overcome me. I walk out into the warm, calm, night air alone. The fresh air revives me. I breathe in the night air, and yes, I am delighted to be alive. I am thrilled to be alive, to be the woman that I always knew I was. I know who I am at last.

I am grateful to be alive, grateful for this safe place to dance. In a year I will have my gender—confirming surgery. In a year, my bodies' chemical make-up, brain, and spirit will be one. I know the surgery will not change my desires, my lust for love and affection. My desires for a warm gentle touch, for soft arms to hold me. I live for the day someone will whisper in my ear "I love you just the way you are." Sometimes I fear that even after my gender correction, I still will just be a lonely transsexual. Deep in my soul I know I have to correct this accident of birth. I have to put my body in tune with my spirit.

I suppose to some people I always will be just a man in a dress. I fear that I will spend my life dancing alone! Floating like a butterfly across the dance room. Dancing alone until the day I fly into the forest, to gently die alone among the wild flowers.

I WAS ALONE,
EVEN WHEN I WAS WITH YOU

From my play, *I was always me*

I live alone now, a prisoner of my own mind, trapped in a room with my reflections. Alone, to share my emotions with myself. It's time to separate what my mind feels from what my soul feels. I am what is commonly called middle-aged; that is, I am no longer young, but not quite old. For the last twenty-five years I have lived with the love of my life. Nineteen years ago my son was born; six and seven years respectively, my daughters blessed my life, a family life gone now, and the question lingers on. "Was I ever really there?" When did I realize that I always was alone?

I was in the Army for three years. In December of 1972, I was discharged from the Army. I left Fort Dix New Jersey, and the army the same way I entered it: alone. Flying from Newark to Boston. faces from the past three years flashed across my mind. Names seemed to be vague. I recalled a year in Vietnam with a strong desire to die and get it over with. I remembered a year and a half in Germany trying to see and taste it all! It is hard; too much booze and drugs have clouded the three years.

Fear of love, fear of my gender, fear of sex; I just realized I have never experienced sex as a sober human being. I wonder if it is any better when alcohol or drugs do not affect your senses. In December of 1972, I arrived back in Boston the night before my grandmother died. I remember the gleam in her eyes; I can honestly say no one, before or since then, has been happier to see me. I promised myself that I would be normal from now on. No more drugs, no more alcohol, no more dresses, and no more gay bars! By the end of that January, I had broken all of the four promises that I had made to myself. It's a pity but if a person cannot be true to himself or herself, whom can they be true to?

I am back in the here and now; In fact I, am back in September of 1998. I am back trying to separate my head from my heart; they are different you know. Sometimes what you feel and what you think you feel are not the same. I just realized that quite recently. Unsure of love, did my wife ever really love me? Did I ever really love her? All I know is we both deeply love our children. I was a child once, a terrorizing experience that I try my best not to reflect on.

I have dyed my hair, slimmed down, and I had my ears pierced. I have reached deep into my soul and found me. Do we have in inner child? I fear we do and I have found mine. Now what do I do with her? To understand my loneness, you would have to know the emotions that I have denied for years. The sense of isolation that has always been with me. I was so young the first time I felt guilt and shame after wearing my sister's clothes. I still have blue eyes, although the Irish gleam seems to have died. "When Irish eyes are crying, the whole world cries." I hope not I prefer to cry alone! I joined the army when I was nineteen years old, the same year I gradated from high school. In high school I was in love with my best friend; sadly, he had a thing for girls. I dated the same girl from JR. High on though the Senior Prom. She still is the one love of my life; she found the woman of her dreams, and is quite happy. I got married and pretended to be happy. Last year my wife told me that she was not happy. She went on to inform me that she was seeking fulfillment elsewhere. I have been sober and drug free for over a year now. It is time to get on with my life, It is time for me to be true to my self. It seems my goal is to find happiness as an unmarried person. If I was not sure if I as happy when I was married how can I tell if I am happy being Unmarried? Shit! I think it is time to take a look at me lifer from the beginning, Maybe I will find me.

Am I old yet?

Am I happily or sadly devoiced?

Am I gay or straight?

Am I too effeminate or too masculine?

As my fiftieth birthday is fast approaching, I think it is time to find some answers in my gender riddle.

MY ELVIS CONNECTION

"Love me tender, Love me sweet'
August 16, 1977, Elvis left us.
"Never let me go"
August 20th 1977 I married the love of my life.
We vowed never to part.
"You made my life complete"
August 20th 1977 our wedding song was "Love me Tender"
We vowed never to part.
"And I love you so, love me true
All my dreams fulfilled, for my darling I love you
And I always will"
August 16, 2002 Elvis's spirit is alive and strong
August 20, my marriage is no more
Dissolved by a court order on July 6, 2000.
"Love me tender, love me long, take me to your heart.
For it's there that I belong and we'll never part."
But part we did, there is no 25 year celebration
Only my loneliness.
We grew apart, you found a new love.
"Love me tender, Love me dear
Tell me you are mine,
I will be yours through all the years
Till the end of time, when at last
My dreams come true."
But part we did, we grew apart
You found a new love.
"Darling this I know happiness will follow you,
Everywhere you go."
Dearest love, my bliss came at a high price
Dearest love, I always will love you tenderly.

FROM CLIPON'S INTO PIERCED EARS

Finding one's true self is not as simple as getting your ears pierced. Yet as silly as it sounds, getting my ears pierced was a huge stepping-stone for me. I was keeping my preference for more feminine attire a deep secret. All the way up to my late forties, guilt and shame still controlled my life. My inner spirit, my very soul was a dark secret. Feeling brave and free shortly after separating from my wife of twenty years, I got two small holes punched into my ears. Yes, I now had pierced ears. I still was known to wear men's attire on a daily basis but now I had studs in both ears!

At that time I was a member of a support group of troubled Vietnam Veterans. A truly manly group of veterans. I had been living with an inner fear for a few years of what these fellow Vietnam Veterans would think of me if they knew the real me. At this time in my life I had reached a milestone; I was sober and drug free for a year. Not since before going to Vietnam had I ever gone over ninety days without some kind of substance abuse.

I always wore clip on earrings when I wanted a certain look, yes clip on earrings were the safe way to go for a certain look. Now clean and sober one sunny day, I walked into a local jewelry store and got my ears pierced. Now even in my male drag outfits, I was wearing earrings. They were just little tiny studs, still I was strong enough to wear them! Almost instantly I became the subject of ridicule. My children called me weird. "Men do not wear earrings on both ears" was the constant refrain. Back then I was not strong enough to say right back WELL! I am not a real man!

The tough insults came from my so-called friends at my Veterans support group. I have to admit to a few other changes during this time frame. I had gone from 178 pounds down to 130 pounds. I also was painting my nails on a regular basis, and my ponytail was getting quite long: and was not always tied up. Yes! The gold studs were a compliment to the new look I was reaching for. By this time I was buying my T-shirts and jeans on the woman's petite racks.

The jokes and stares were nasty and mean spirited; my support group was no longer offering me any support. Instead they were loudly asking personal question.

> What is wrong with John?
> Does he have AIDS?
> Is he gay?
> Is he going to show up in a dress next week?
> Is he going to have his penis cut off?
> Christ! All I did was get my ears pierced!

You know, at this point in my life I realized that a sex realignment surgery would not be such a bad thing. I was now wearing silver rings on both hands. I was wearing bracelets, necklaces, and dresses every day. In fact, my male wardrobe was rapidly disappearing.

The day came when I had to face reality. Why was I going to a support group that offered me no support? With my VA therapist's support, I left the group. I was now strong enough now to go out and find a gender support group. I give thanks to my Veterans support group; they may not realize it but they gave me the confidence to be my true self. My will to be my true self came from that group of fellow proud Vietnam veterans. They gave me the courage to stop hiding who I was and to stop living the lie that had controlled my life. That group taught me to have pride in who I was, and I was a proud trans woman

It was that simple decision to stop wearing clip on earrings at night but to wear pieced earrings day and night that released me from my cocoon. My wings are colorful and opened wide. I am flying with the breeze, gliding through the sun's rays.

WHAT MATTERS NOW?

I begin with this glow, a feeling of completeness. For the first time in my life, my body, my soul, and my spirit, my mind are one. But what matters now? My life goes on. I am still the loving parent of three beautiful children. A 20-year-old son totally accepting of my new found bliss. My two young daughters still my main concern. They mean so much to me.

Two weeks before my surgery, I take them aside separately, and try to get them to open up to me. I have been out of their house for over two years now. For a year and a half another person has been sleeping with my wife.

What matters now? I have this miracle: A chance through surgery to put my life long nightmare to an end. Am I being selfish? My daughters' well being is what matters now.

I tell my loving Melissa that I am still her father. I always will be. She has spent the last three years watching her father's rebirth as a woman. Every Wednesday night I take them out, I have not missed one yet.

What matters now? For the last time I am letting my babies control me, giving them more power then I should. I trust my years of home schooling them have made them wise. What matters now?.

I cannot have this surgery, if in any way it will come between us; I tell my loving Melissa. She smiles gazing into my tearful eyes. "Dad" she says "I know you love me. I know you are happy, and that is all that I need to know." You know I would go back for you, I whisper. She says, "Back to being sad, drunk, and angry all the time" We finish our burgers and shakes. This is all that matters now. Now I ask my younger daughter the same question.

I invite my little computer expert over to my apartment. She is working on my "I WAS ALWAYS ME" web site. It is not long before she spills out that Melissa has told her about my upcoming surgery, and of my question to her.

What matters now? You matter now I insure her. Jeanette who. From day one has been crying out, I what my dad back, now looks at me with a smile. She is just twelve years old and a spitting image of me. Curly hair and big blue eyes behind her glasses.

With the wisdom of much more years then she has, she says, "I know you are my dad, and I know you love me." I know you will still be my dad even after the surgery. We talk about a move she saw called "The adventures of Sebastian Cole". I reassure her that it was just a movie. In real life no one dies from intersex surgery.

She gives me a big hug! This is all that matters now!

MY LAST GENDER WALL

My voice is my last gender wall; I have torn all the other gender walls down. Those short manly haircuts have been replaced, with long, flowing curly touched up hair. That flat hairy chest replaced, thanks to hormones, with small perky breasts. That huge manly beer gut is gone! Thank the Goddesses. My fat mass has shifted, my hips have emerged. Yes, that wall of gender denial has been torn down.

My face, now soft and hairless, is smiling now, the life long sadness gone. My hands were one of those walls, perpetually dirty and callused. A part of the gender wall now clean, soft, with long painted nails. My legs, once hairy and always hidden under my pants, now are hairless; they now are soft and shapely. They now are tanned from the exposure to the sun, another gender wall torn down.

Oh, how I have torn down all those gender walls right down to my feet, yes, even my feet, too, are usually naked in the Florida sun showing off my tastes in toenail coloring!.

My gender walls OH how they have all been torn down
Well, all but one. My Voice, My Voice
This deep voice, this vocal expression that is part of me.
I keep this wall, I keep this wall.
I have said it is the last trait of my children's father.
I have said that I am too lazy to do voice exercises
My voice is me; I just need to keep some of me!
My last gender wall, I keep it up
I really do not know why.

PIECES OF ME

Pieces of me are scattered all over Mother Earth.
Pieces of me scarred by incest, scarred by childhood rape.
Pieces of me scattered all over Mother Earth.
Pieces of me scarred by the adolescent gender wars
Pieces of me buried with my father and brother.
Pieces of me breathing in my mothers and siblings souls.
Pieces of me scarred by a long ago war
Pieces of me buried with the souls that no medic could save
Killed in a senseless war.
Pieces of me scattered all over mother Earth.
Piece by piece my soul dying in a lonely marriage.
Pieces of me, pieces of me flowering in my children.
Pieces of me forever lost in the gender wars.
Oh, Yes! A man can fake an orgasm!
Pieces of me scattered all over Mother Earth
Pieces of me, pieces of me
My penis, my vagina, my maleness, my femaleness.
Pieces of me, pieces of me scattered all over Mother Earth.
Pieces of me, pieces of me
All of these pieces at last fitting into a whole me.
Pieces of me under Farther Sky, whole and complete, under Farther Sky.
Pieces of me, pieces of me together whole at last on Mother Earth.

WHEN WILL IT BE MY TIME?

During my adolescence, I was taught boys chase girls, and girls chase after boys. Boys grow up to marry women, and girls grow up and marry men. During my adolescence, I was taught that boys hide their emotions and inner fears. It was beaten into me that I was a boy. "Stop doing that! You are a boy, not a girl!" I was taught to hide my inner desires; Boys do not feel that way about other boys.

During my teenage years I was occupied with thoughts of how to avoid going into the army. Throughout those years I worked hard at not being my true self. All I heard was my, what a young man you are becoming. In my late teens I started to believe the lie; I was becoming a man. At the age of nineteen I did the manly thing and joined the army. "What a brave young man, "I heard.

In my twenties I got married; all men get married in there twenties or so my mother told me. The same mother that had my long curly hair cut off. The same mother that kept telling me that I was a boy, not a girl. My wife told me that I have to stop wearing dresses, and sleeping in silk nightgowns. I was a husband now! When I became a father, I was told "you have to dress and act more manly; you are a father now." As my adult years went by all I heard was "For the sake of the kids," walk and talk and dress like a real man." I am in my mid-life now; I no longer have a wife. My children now know the true me. The act in that life-long play has come to an end. The second act of this play I call my life has began. At the age of fifty, I am free at last!

Now my little brother looks at me with disgust, my mother and baby sister ask me to stay away from them.

Oh! Dear Goddess, when will it be my time to live?

CHASING BUTTERFLIES IN COSTA RICA

From my play: *"I WAS ALWAYS ME"*

When I was a young girl, I spent a summer with my father in Costa Rica. He was a Botanist studying in the rain forest. I got to spend the summer chasing and playing among the most beautiful butterflies in the world. I love butterflies; their metamorphosis from caterpillar to butterfly is one of Mother Earth's great wonders. The unattractive caterpillar weaves itself into a cocoon, takes a long nap, and then breaks out as a thing of beauty; a multi-colored butterfly.

In the rain forest of Costa Rica the biggest and most colorful butterflies are a sight to behold! You can close your eyes and hear the sounds of fluttering wings. The sounds of birds singing, and the sight of colorful butterflies make for a paradise here on Earth.

Reality does suck! I love dreaming. In reality, I never was a little girl. In reality, I was a little boy. I never spent a summer in the rain forest. Or was ever close to my father. Thanks to my father, though I did get to spend a year in the rain forest of Vietnam. I cannot recall seeing any butterflies that year. I always pretended to be a boy in hopes of making my father like me. He always told me to stop acting like a sissy. He always made fun of the way I dressed and walked. He was forever yelling at me "get a haircut. You look like a girl!" I got haircuts for my father and acted like a boy for my father's love, although it never came.

In 1969 I pretended I was a man and joined the Army, with delusions of winning my father's love and respect. I was not a pretend boy any more; I was a pretend man, a dangerous thing to be in 1969. I was a caterpillar without the knowledge of how to weave a cocoon.

Fantasy is so much more satisfying than reality! When I was a little girl, chasing butterflies, I would dream my life away about growing up to be a beautiful woman. I daydreamed my life away, safe in the sanctuary of the library. No one made fun of me there. I could read what I felt like reading. I could dream my dreams. I learned about butterflies and Costa Rica in the library.

All dreams end with a sudden dose of reality. I learned all about reality in Vietnam. I hated the Army. They tried their best to make a man out of me. In 1970, I was 20 years old, and I was 5'6" weighing 126 pounds. Even in Vietnam I still was daydreaming about growing up to be a beautiful woman.

In Vietnam I was a seeker of peace, by way of death, though I did not find either peace or death. I am home in NH; where I spend as much time as possible walking in New England's peaceful woods. Now In spite of my father, in spite of the Army, in spite of the war; I did grow up to be a beautiful woman. I did find out how to weave a cocoon; I did break out as a colorful butterfly! I still daydream about running through the rain forests of Costa Rica chasing butterflies, Wearing a long flowing dress that is as colorful as the butterflies. I was looking at some old pictures the other day. Boy, did I look lost and sad in that Army uniform. Some nights I still wake up from nightmares of my childhood. Some nights are full of dreams of those long ago nights in Vietnam. My worst fears come back then. Fears that I would not die in Vietnam, fears that I would have to return to the world with my dark secret! That DARK SECRET! I am not a man! Enough of that. Today the reality is I am a woman. Reality does not suck after all! I did grow up to be a beautiful woman. I do chase butterflies through the woods of NH in long flowing colorful skirts!.

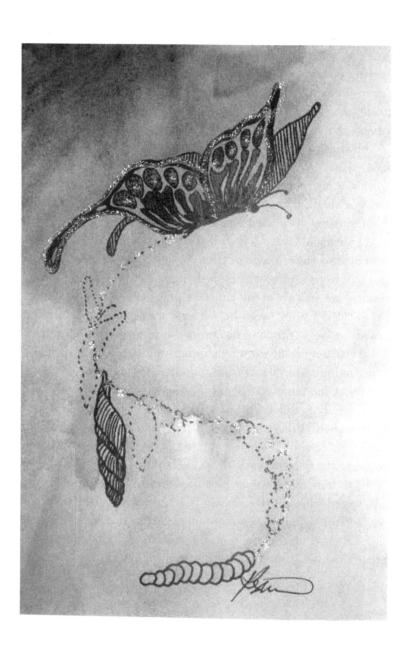

BOOK FOUR

FINDING, ME

MY LIFE AS JANICE JOSEPHINE CARNEY

I AM STILL ME

JOHN JOSEPH CARNEY OR JANICE JOSIPHINE CARENY,

From, my play "*I was always me*"

I feel I have an obligation to explain myself to my family, so here I go:

One of those silly sayings in A.A. is "Are you comfortable in your skin?" After two years of going to A.A. meetings, my answer to that question was "NO!" I still felt awkward and out of place. I have felt this way all of my life. Now, for the first time in my life I was looking inward, and asking myself, why? Having a gender was the answer.

What makes me happy? What would make me feel comfortable? What can make me feel normal? Having a gender was the answer. Yes! As strange as it sounds the freedom to dress the way I felt like was the key. Yes, I was a strange man who had the inspirations and emotions of a woman. Maybe I was not even a man. YES! I was happy and normal wearing feminine attire, with painted nails, with long flowing hair. When I am called Ma'm, I am comfortable in my skin. It took me forty-eight years to find this tranquility; why is it so bad?

Did anyone ever notice how lonely and isolated I was as a child? Did any one ever notice my constant struggle to fit in? Did any one ever notice my preference for girl's clothes; did any one ever notice the hours of isolation that I spent in the Bunker Hill Library? Did any one ever notice what books I took out of the library bus when we lived in the Columbia Point Housing Project? I wanted to live in that French orphanage with Madeline and all the other girls!

A great deal of my childhood is a dark haze, yet I do remember consistently daydreaming about growing up into womanhood. I recall always trying to hide my penis. I am simply trying to explain that this is not just some kind of mid-life crisis; I am not overreacting to the end of my 20-year marriage. I am at last dealing with a Internal crisis that I have struggled with my whole life.

I now have the freedom to live my life as I wish, and I am going to follow my inner spirit. I no longer can hold my soul as a hidden captive.

All through high school I was in a constant state of confusion. Unsure of my sexuality, unsure of my gender, daydreaming about disappearing and then reappearing as a woman, and secretly wearing women's clothes whenever I had the chance. Recently I had a conversation with the only two girls that I dated in high school. One, who is now in a long-term relationship, with another women. She told me that I always would be in her heart. She said that I used to have a soft, gentle almost feminine way about me that she loved.

She was glad that I was getting it back. She thought that side of me had died in Vietnam, was how she put it. I had lunch with the other one as Janice twice last month; she said she has never seen me more relaxed. "You were always more like a girl friend" she said. My closest male friend from high school has not talked to me since I let him know how I really felt about him!

Did anyone ever notice my feminine appearance during my last year in high school? Twice that year I ended up at the hospital emergency ward after being assaulted due to my feminine appearance. I felt free and happy in tight bell-bottom jeans, colorful shirts, with beads around my neck and wrist. My long hippy hair all over my face! I was always on the edge of being the real me, yet I was too full of shame and guilt to let my spirit free.

It was that shame and guilt that led me to join the Army In 1969. I thought the Army would change me. They would turn me into a real man that everyone would be proud of. In 1972, 1973, didn't anyone notice how quickly that old feminine appearance returned? Did anyone notice my internal struggle over what gender I was? For a period I found happiness and lived as the woman that I had dreamed of being. Then the shame and guilt overwhelmed me. I was just a man in a dress!! Most of those nights that I lived alone on Cross Street, I cried myself to sleep. Was I a macho beer guzzling Vietnam Veteran or was I a budding drag queen?

Had I the strength back then to put the booze down, the raging drag queen would have won out. If I had listened to my inner spirit way back then, I would not have tried marriage as another attempt at being the man that I could never be. Drugs [some prescribed, some not] and alcohol denied me access to the spirit that the Goddess had put in my soul.

Did anyone see how lost I was, in alcohol and drugs for the twenty years of my marriage? Did I ever look happy during those years? Did I ever seem relaxed during all those years? Comfortable in my skin, did I ever appear comfortable during all those years? What is normal? I do not know, all I know is all those years I felt out of place and awkward. I guess that is abnormal. Let me try to define normal. Normal is being outside What you are inside; when you hide what you are inside, out of shame and guilt, You are abnormal!

I have known since early in my childhood that inside I was a woman, my inner spirit, my soul was and is that of a woman's. There are no words that can explain the pain that I lived with knowing this. Thinking that I had no choice but to live my whole life as a man. When I moved back to Massachusetts. Two years ago, I vowed that I would be myself from now on. Back to those silly A.A. sayings: "To thy own self be true." The truth is I am a woman and I always have been.

The first morning I walked up to the Dunkan Donut's in comfortable clothes, I felt my inner spirit being released. No shame, no guilt, I was just being the woman I was born to be. This time if any one was going to punch me in the face I was going to fight back! I felt like I was back in high school.

I let my inner spirit out to my VA doctors. I opened up to a gender support group. I got a new doctor in Boston. I went to my

A.A. meeting with painted nails, long flowing hair, and just the right amount of makeup.

I spent a year in Malden Massachusetts Growing into the woman I always know I would be. The following year, in December I moved back to New Hampshire as Janice Josephine Carney. Janice was the name on my checkbook, as well as Joplin's name, so I took it. Josephine is what my mother called me when I was a small child with long curly hair, so I took it! I am Janice Josephine Carney. Today every one in my life knows me as Janice Josephine. Just a name, yet whenever I hear" Janice Josephine" my face lights up. Yes! That's me. I am alive, I am happy; I do not hear John any more. On the rare occasion I do hear John It is like a flash back to a dark and lonely distant past.

In my first year back in NH my doctor put me on a hormone balancing treatment. I made contact with Dr. Biber in Colorado; He was to be the doctor that would correct my birth defect. In my second year back In NH, I did go to Colorado and I did have my body aligned with my spirit. Yes, it was an expensive and painful surgery, yet well worth every dime and every bit of the pain! I am at peace with my inner spirit!

This has turned into a long and rambling letter, but I am trying to explain my fifty years on the Earth. My goal is at the age of 55 to be just another middle-aged lady living in Clearwater, Florida. I no longer have any shame or guilt over who I am. The down side is my family having a massive amount of shame and guilt over who I am. Why are they not happy that a lonely, angry, alcoholic, human being is now a happy, sober human being?

REWALKING MAIN STREET USA,

(MY THREE YEARS IN THE FOURTH GRADE.)

As a liberated fifty-one year old transsexual, I recently attended a speak out* training session. It was held at The Bunker Hill Community College in Charlestown. On an unexpectedly beautiful morning in October, I pulled into the Sullivan Square. parking lot. I recalled living in a house right here on this spot where I was parking. Looking around I envisioned the Stickney and Poor Spice Company that used to be across the street. I turned around, looking up across the parking lot half expecting to see the old Sullivan Square MTA Station! They both are long gone just like my childhood. I stood in the spring-like rain, closing my eyes. I swear I smelled the mixed spices and heard the rattle of the overhead train. For a moment all that loneliness of being in a big Irish Catholic family came back to haunt me.

In a daze, I headed towards the old Celtic Tavern instead of towards the train station. On the corner was the old Charlestown Clinic and the Celtic Tavern, now the Teamster's Clinic, and an upscale bistro. I stopped in front of the old tavern, gazing at the door, flashing back to that lonely boy looking for his father. I recalled the day I had my leg stiched in the old clinic, the results of leaping off a roof in my fantasy world of Peter Pan and Tinkebell. My father, dead from years of alcohol and tobacco abuse, lingered on my mind. I wondered: if he were alive, would he accept me for the woman I have grown into? Sighing, I crossed over Cambridge Street and across Rutherford Avenue gazing over at the fenced in rotary. In the days of my youth, the overhead train station and tracks cast a massive shadow over this area; I would play in the long grass in the rotary. There in the grass I explored sex with other boys. In the

foggy morning I could see the old park in the distance. The Neck
is a park that sits on the edge of the Boston Harbor.

It was when I was living in this area that my older brother
began sneaking into my bed at night. My fears and tears run
together as I stand here recalling a childhood of darkness. Gazing
across the early morning fog at the park where I did not learn how
to play baseball, I recall how I learned to be invisible in the shadows
of the oil tankers unloading in the Everett Terminal.

I remember spending days, never being picked to play ball,
only to wonder off, lying in the grass feeling invisible, never a part
of any thing! On this day, I am part of something, and I live in
New Hampshire miles away from my childhood. Crossing
Rutherford Avenue, I head toward Main Street and my destination.
As I cross the railroad tracks under the shadow of the old Scheraffts
building, I paused to look up to the top of Bunker Hill. So many
memories buried in a black abyss of my mind! Such was my
childhood! Glaring up Bunker Hill, I flash back to my three years
in the fourth grade. The constant moving, so many houses, yet
never a home. At the bottom of the hill, a huge local garden is
flourishing where the Bunker Hill School once stood. Up at the
top of the hill stands the old St Frances Catholic School.

Somewhere in between the houses and High Street sits the
new Warren School replacing, one of my schoolyards of fear. Turning
down Main Street, it seemed eerie and quiet. The sounds of the
overhead trains having long gone. Somewhere in the back of my
head I could still hear the loud screeching and rattling of the
overhead trains. At the end of Main Street sits the old Harvard
School, now an elderly housing complex. At all these schools I did
a stretch of time in the fourth grade. Three years, a short period,
just time, no learning, no bonding, and no growth!

As I walk down Main Street. I can feel a tear coming down my
cheek. A tear for the loneliest boy in the world. The boy that was
a girl, and no one noticed! As I walk down Main Street, I feel a
shiver as I remember the first time I felt that pain!

That pain as my brother rolled me over on my side and
penetrated me. So many memories, so much pain. Turning

backward toward Sullivan Square, I remember the house on Caldwell Street where we lived when I went to St Frances. I Stand on Main Street looking across at where the triple-decker once stood, the one I lived in when I cut my leg. I think I was going to the Bunker Hill School that year. I remember living on the third floor eyeball-to-eyeball with the overhead train. Looking back at the Sullivan Square parking lot, I try to remember what school I went to when we lived in that house; I cannot recall. What house did I live in when I was in the fourth grade at the Warren School? I just cannot recall. I have memories of always running from something, always being chased, always being made fun of! Memories of stuttering, constant fear, blurred vision; always being made fun of!

I have memories of living in Somerville, and being put in the fifth grade, of having a teacher work with my speech problems; it was then that my brother moved out of my life. Here I got my first pair of glasses. As I turned down Main Street and continue my walk, I smile I have found a pride in this person I have become. I have confidence in who I am. I am a complete human being at last. Intersex surgery, gender-altering surgery, sex reassignment surgery. Call it what you like. I am corrected. I am a woman today. I have a glow about me, I am happy to be alive. I am walking down the main street of the town of my youth with pride.

Looking across Rutherford Avenue where the Hood Milk plant was, I remember when my brother and I used to fill recyclable glass milk bottles up with left over milk in returned bottles to take home. I, Janice Josephine Carney, can actually look back and smile. I solved the riddle, the gender riddle, I found me, the me that I never had as a child.

No, I never had any reassignment, no alteration, no change, I was me all along! John Joseph always was Janice Josephine! I never was allowed to be me, all those childhood years living in fear. Today I am glowing in the warmth of this spring-like October morning. I cannot recall such a beautiful morning in any childhood years here in Charlestown. Half way down Main Street I come to the street where my grandmother lived. I recall a wise old woman who had a sense, of who I was, the only person who had a clue. I can see her smile, feel her touch; sense her being, as I walk across Main Street. Yes, Grandma, I survived the Army, I survived the war, I overcame it all, all that denial to stand here today. I know Grandma is looking upon me, seeing my long curly hair, and long skirt blowing, in the early morning breeze. I never felt such a strong agreement with life. Yes, I am glad to be alive!

Heading back down Main Street, I walk past the Russell Jr. High School. I went there In Nov. 1963, at the age of 13. I do not remember where I lived, at the time. I remember not long after running away from home and moving in with my sister in Somerville. I sold newspapers that day, EXTRA EXTRA PRESIDENT KENNEDY SHOT IN DALLAS, that was my last year living in Charlestown, my last year of running, of living in constant fear.

I am near the end of Main Street; at what was one time the Thompson Square MTA stop. I close my eyes and I swear I hear the overhead trains screeching on their brakes as they enter the station. I open my eyes where the old Thompson Sq Theater used to be it is a bank now. Crossing Main Street I can see the old Bunker Hill Boys Club. Looking up the side street across from the new shopping center, I can see the old library. Always afraid to go home, these were the places I felt safe during those dark years. Strange, though, I cannot remember what triple-decker I lived in at this end of Main Street. I recall living on Russell Street, a side street of Bunker Hill. I know we lived in a house right here in an alley. These houses are gone now. As I enter the shopping plaza, I now remember here, right here, when I was going to the Harvard School, my first year in the fourth grade, here is where that house was, here is where the rapes, the incest started!

Here is where the fear of going to school, the fear of staying home, the fear of who or what I was began.

I wish I had screamed out, I am not boy! I know there is something wrong. The pedophile in my life stopped my growth, ended my natural being. Now I stand in front of the Bunker Hill Community College, I stand tall and proud. I have just walked through the maze that was my childhood. The sun has broken through. The early morning rain has stopped. I stand here a proud transsexual, no shame, no guilt, here with a smile, here with a glow about me! I, Janice Josephine Carney, am ready for some SPEAK OUT TRAINING!

I survived those three years in the fourth grade. I am here to show "TRANSJAN" ** to try to show young transgendered people that there is a way to be your true self. To let others know they can find their true gender. Right here, off Main Street USA we G, L, Bi and transgendered souls are learning from each other today!

- Speak Out is an organization of GLBT speakers In Boston.
- Transjan is a short documentary on my transition; that I screen for educational purposes.

I LEFT THREE PIECES OF MY HEART BEHIND

I left three pieces of my heart behind;
    Yet it was time to move on
I left three pieces of my heart behind
    Yet it was time for me to go
I left three pieces of my heart behind:

    Yet it was time for me to grow.
My heart is free and glowing,
    This adventure called life is bringing
Me much joy
I left three pieces of my heart behind
    One' my loving son SHAUN, my pride and joy;
Happy Valentine' days Shaun know on this day set aside for
Love that I love you
    Two: Melissa, my beautiful dreamy eyed Melissa, please keep
e-mailing me about your dreams and hopes. I will always be here
waiting to hear from you. Happy Valentines Day. Love dad
    Three: my baby binnie the kid, oh how I miss you! Dear
Jeanette, please e mail me, and tell me
What is going on in that wonderful mind of yours.
Happy Valentines Day to you, with all my love.
I left three pieces of my heart behind
    Yet it was time for me to move on.
I left three pieces of my heart behind;
    Yet it was time for me to go,
I left three pieces of my heart behind

Yet it was time for me to grow
My heart is mixed with gladness and sadness
This adventure called life has brought me
Much sadness.
YET I have found a measure of peace here
In the Fla. Sun
Happy Valentine to the three pieces of my heart
That I left behind. Love dad
PS; Have Ma cash this check for
Valentines day pizza.

THE QUEEN OF P TOWN

From my play, "*I was always me*"

I saw her on the first day; her face was aglow. Her long blonde hair blazing in the sun, Her perfectly shaped tan body on roller blades buzzing down the Center of Commercial Street. She waved both of her hands at me with a radiant smile and full of enthusiasm. She yelled as she rolled by: "Sweetheart, I'll see you at the A club tonight." I spent the rest of the day wondering: Does she like me? Does she greet all the new girls in town that warmly? What to wear tonight soon over took my thoughts.

The sunshine turned to moonshine. A delightful crescent moon replaced the blazing sun. I was dressed up and in search of the Queen of P town. The music and dance lights bring my tired soul to life. The dance floor is were my spirit shines.

I felt a gentle touch on my shoulder, a gentle touch of a fellow tired soul. A soft hand, a gentle touch. "Hi sweetheart, I am so happy that you found the club." Her long blonde hair blazing, even in the dark club. *I am pretty, I am pretty, dam it,* echoed across the club. For the rest of the night we were girlfriends sharing a secret intimacy. The night ended way too soon, and I lost her in the existing crowed.

Sunday morning as I was searching for breakfast I heard her delightful voice: "over here sweet heart over here." Her blonde hair blowing in the early morning breeze. I eagerly joined her for eggs and girl chat. She did not look as bubbly.

Her face, still soft and pretty, was being over taken with the shadow of facial hair. A sadness over took her face. "I wish that I could be me forever" she said with a tear in her eye.

The Queen of P town was a weekend queen. Her face lit up when I told her that I was starting hormone treatment. I was going to be free of this ugly facial hair. She exclaimed, "I wish I was you." For the first time in my life some one wished that they were me! The queen Of P town was going home to her family, home to her job. She smiled wearily saying, "This queen is going back in the closet." "I wish that I could be you." She kissed me on the lips, as she said goodbye. I ran by fingers through her long blonde hair as we ended our embrace.

I watched her wonder off as the sun reflected of her hair. Sad, yet happy; I can be me every day of the week. I can be me every hour of every day. I can be the Queen of Derry New Hampshire

WHAT ARE YOU?

A couple of weeks ago, I was dancing with a delightful woman in
  the Vixen club.
I walked her home, holding her hand. Along the way she stopped,
  turned to me.
Looking me in the eyes she asked:
    What are you?
    I replied. I am queer!
What is more queer then a man who denies his birth, and is reborn
  as a woman!
I am a queer! What are you?
    Are you gay?
No! I am not a man! No! I am not gay!
    Are you straight? What are you?
I am queer! I am queer!
    Straight! The world will not allow me to be, dear!
What are you! She still asks.
    I am a queer, I still respond.
Are you bisexual? What are you?
    I could be bi sexual I guess, but I have this fear of men.
That is a drawback to being Bi sexual, I guess.
    What are you? What are you?
I am queer, I am queer!!!!
    What are you? what are you?
    I am a queer.
I am a lesbian. Is that queer enough for you dear?
    I am a transsexual lesbian! I am lonely, please let me in!

I DANCE ALONE

I danced with a man tonight, I do not know why!
I danced with a woman last week, I know why!
Mostly I dance alone.
Every now and then I go to a single's dance,
I do not know why!
Every now and then, I go to a gay club
I know why!
I feel nervous and odd,
Dancing in a man's embrace,
I feel snug and in sync,
When I am dancing in a woman's embrance!
I danced with a man tonight!
An attempt to fit in to societies' norms, I guess!
I danced with a woman, last week,
An attempt to find peace and contentment, I guess
Mostly I dance alone, I do not know why!

A SMALL BOX OF BOOKS

ON 25,March 2003 there was a murder in Gulfport Florida! I often drive over to Gulfport when I am stressed out and need a little peace and serenity. Gulfport is a reposeful. hamlet; it is my oasis from a desert of loneness. Java Jane's was my destination; peaceful conversation with an iced coffee was my goal.

As I parked my car across the street from my favorite coffee shop, I saw a commotion in front of the courtyard leading into Java Jane's. There were a few men waving fanatically, as I crossed the street. As I approached the courtyard, a man zealously waved at me to cross to the other side of the street.

I glanced down at the sidewalk to see a man. His head was covered with a blood soaked t-shirt! My stomach and head begin to spin as I watched him gasping his last breath, as his last ounce of blood stained the courtyard.

As I turned to cross the street, a police officer was racing towards me screaming, "Which way did the bad guy go?" One of the men described the shooter and the car he was driving. The police officer was passing it on through the dispatcher. Another Gulfport police car was in quick pursuit.

I walked down Beach Boulevard, dazed, at how close I had been to another man being shot in the head! Oh yes! I have been here before!

Here was in Vietnam so many years ago. Here was a housing project in Boston so many years ago.

Today, here right, this moment, in this town that has become my haven, why, why does this male violence confront me again?

With my head spinning, my stomach ready to explode, I made it into the used bookstore. I was gasping for air and close to a state of shock, as the bookstore owner brought me a glass of water and led me to a chair. My past, my here and now, my future were all colliding. My childhood in Boston's housing projects, my year in Vietnam, my faith, and my bliss lying in another pool of blood right here on the courtyard of Java Jane's.

Here in my beloved Gulfport, I am put to another test of my strength! I stood in a shocked state. The images of my past life, of the past few nights of cable TV. Death in Vietnam, death in Iraq, death on the curb of a street in a Boston housing project, death in the courtyard of Java Jane's; blood every where I looked! I saw those terrified eyes of the women from an army reserve unit, now a POW.

I recalled how close I was to being in her shoes, so many years ago.

What am I to learn from all of this? There I was sitting in a corner of this tiny bookstore in Gulfport: so afraid that my soul is losing the fight for bliss. The bookstores owner's voice guides me to the back room of the store. Here "Sit down and look at this small box of books that were just dropped off," she says.

My soul, my sprit both so scarred! A small box of books. I find a copy of:

"*The Chalice and the Blade*" by Riane Eisler
"*Care of the soul*" by Thomas Moore
Two books that I already have read, books that have enlightened me.

A book oh the her/history of ancient Goddess, books on ancient spiritual traditions.

I find Kay Turner's'" *Beautiful Necessity*" the art and meaning of women's altars.

The "*Storyteller's Goddess*" Tales of the

What am I to learn from all of this?
From a small box of books, some one dropped off, meant for me.

From all of these sights, sounds, and smells, these memories,
all things I was meant to witness
What am I to learn from all of this?
My Soul grows. My scars will heal,
A death in Gulfport; another piece of my life.
Maybe I will find the answer in this small box of books!

Written on March 26, 2003

MINUTES FROM MIDNIGHT

It's minutes from midnight
The end of another day
Another day spent all alone
Just minutes away from midnight.
Morning coffee all alone,
With the St Petersburg Times
A swim in the complex pool
Early afternoon conversation
With the women of the View and there guest
Lunch all alone at my favorite restaurant.
A diet Coke or a diet Pepsi
Possibly sweet ice tea
Differently not a glass of wine!
Wine and loneness do not mix well.
Dinner all alone at my second favorite restaurant
A sunset walk along a Gulf beach
Internet exchanges, from the closest
Things to friends that I have.

Minutes from midnight
I am ending another day spent alone
No drowning of my emotions with a bottle of wine
Good old sobriety, is my closest friend
Shell I say goodnight to Ted Koppel, Jay Leno or David Lettermen?
Seconds away from midnight.
I have a grand father as well as a grandmother clock
At midnight I have dueling gongs
Another night sleeping alone.
Minutes after midnight
The air is still
The silent night echoes my loneliness.
Peaceful slumber will lead to other midnights.
Midnights that will end
Days not so full of emptiness.

THE BIG BANG

Most post-op woman are over-eager, as soon as the pain from the intersex surgery has faded and their energy comes back, to test out their new vaginas; an instant orgasm check! I am waiting for the Big Bang! Yes! The Big Bang. For me the intimacy of a relationship is a key part of the Big Bang. For me the Big Bang will come as a gift from the Goddess, it will be a kindred spirit with a gentle touch.

Oh! The Big Bang will come with eyes that touch my eyes, with a hand that will hold my hand in full view of conservative Florida. YES! My Big Bang will come with my kindred spirit,
> With eyes melting into mine,
> With that soft gentle touch,
> With that soft gentle embrace,
> With a smile that, will make me melt.

Yes! My Big Bang will come
Yes! That special Woman,
Yes! That special kindred Spirit,
Yes that special soft Touch.
Our spirits will grow together, with out fear, our hands,
Our eyes touching as we glow in the Florida sun
Our Big Bang will come when the moment is meant to be.
Our touch, our kiss, our sexual gratifications,
Will be more then a night of selfish passions.
No small bang for me; I will want for the Big Bang!

Yes: knowing that I am in the right embrace,
    Knowing that we will blow out the candles together,
    Our eyes touching,
    Our breasts touching,
    Our hips touching
    Our thighs touching
    Our toes interweaved, yes! This will be our Big Bang, for a Big Bang requires two souls, a small bang is a selfish gratification, not for me.

My kindred spirit is here in Florida seeking her Big Bang; our paths will cross, our souls, will touch.

We will have our Big Bang!

UNDER THE INFLUENCE OF THE FULL MOON

The moon, be it full, cut in half or in a beautiful cresset glow,
    Has an influence on me.
Close your eyes; breathe in the night air.
Listen, and you will feel the influence of the full moon.
    Vision, Lake Winnipesaukee,
The moon is full,
    Reflecting ever so peacefully on the lake; it is midnight.
Lake Winnipeasaukee, on an October midnight.
    A full harvest moon,
Listen for the ancient drumbeats,
Listen to the sound of ancient rattles.
For on this night the spirits of our ancestors and the living share
    the drumming and the shaking of rattles.
Listen to the sounds of the drums, and rattles in the night.
    Feel the heat of the bonfire on an October new England night.
    The flames, shooting up higher, and higher; toward the full moon.
The flickering fire sparks glowing under the full moon.
As I dance around the fire, I have never been more alive.
    The Full moon, the lake, the drums,
The rattles, the fire, my ancestors, my new family of friends,
We are one.
Can you vision? Can you feel the magic?
Oh! Indeed this is a magical night, the magic of the ancient Medicine
    Wheel.

The influence of the moon,
Brings out a long dead spirit from my soul.
The full moon calling to me, Dance, Dance, Dance
                    Live, live, live
On this night all of John's pain is gone.
I am dancing under a full moon, my long skirt flowing in the
    night air
Dancing around the fire, the drums and rattles moving through
    my soul.
The full moon has influenced me, I am alive,
My spirit reflecting of the bon fire
My spirit reflecting of the full moon,
My spirit reflecting of lake Winnipesaukee.
I am the spirit of Cedar Raven.
I am alive; I am dancing with my two spirited ancestors
        Janice Josephine Carney AKA Cedar Raven

THEY DIED AS THEY LIVED

Laden and laleh
They lived their lives as one
Yet they were two.
Two compete women conjoined at the head
Two separate women living as one
Living all those years with a passion to separate
Laden and Laleh
OH! How I can relate to their plight
For I lived fifty years as two genders
For fifty years, I so wanted to separate
John and Janice
Two separate genders conjoined
They lived their life as male
Declared male at birth, yet female
John and Janice
Spending a lifetime wanting to release
That female spirit within that male body
Laden and Laleh.
They died as they lived, together
Laden and Laleh
They both agreed
To separate was worth dying for.
Janice and john
We agreed to separate was worth dying for
The night before my intersex surgery
I lay in the hospital bed full of fears of a long and painful surgery
A chance to separate, a chance to live
To live as one gender
This is worth dying for

Laden and Laleh
They only had a few hours of separation
Well worth dying for
Oh yes!
If my heart stopped beating, if my lungs stopped breathing
If I only had a few hours of separation
Only a few hours being whole
A whole woman, one soul, one body, one brain,
Hormonally balanced
Oh yes! It would have been worth dying for.
Laden, Laleh, and John, where separate souls, gone now
Yes laden or Laleh would have died for the other to live
So John died so that Janice could live.
Together John/Janice where on the edge of a slow death from alcohol/
    drug abuse
Janice, I pray can do enough living for John, Laden and Laleh.

POLITICAL PASSIONS VS.

PERSONAL SHYNESS

My passion for social justice
My passion for transgender liberation.
Far outweigh my passion for personal pleasures.
My shyness, OH! Yes I am shy
So shy and unsure of myself.
My passion for social justice
My passion for Transgender Liberation
These passions overpower my shyness.
No! I am not shy about Transgender Liberation
My loneness, my shyness
My unsure ness, my insecurities are real.
As real as my passion to end the suicides
      To end the violence
      To end the discrimination
As real as my passion for Transgender Liberation,
OH! How this passion flows through my veins
Oh! How this passion makes my voice loud and strong
My loneness my unsure ness, my shyness
These things lie under the shadows of my passions.
My passion for social justice
My passion for Transgender Liberation
Every day my soul bleeds
    Another suicide
    Another beating
    Another murder

Were is the outrage?
We are blessed with our two spirits
Yet cursed with bodies that we cannot live in!
Our very existence a outrage to so many.
My passions, My passions, My passions
Oh! How I can speak up,
Oh! How I can show my outrage.
Oh! How I can give all I have
My loneliness, my unsure ness, my shyness
Oh how my needs go on intended.

HATE VS. LOVE; IN A MOMENT

Let me melt into you
Hold me, just let
Me melt into you.
Hold me, absorb me
For in this moment
I am part of you,
Just let me melt into you,
Just absorb me
Just hold me,
Let me believe,
That this moment will last forever.
For it has been so long,
So long since I have been touched like this.
For it has been so long,
So long since I have touched someone like this.
This human touch
Our skins, becoming one skin
Oh! It has been so long
So long since I have tasted, love
Let me melt into you,
Let me absorb into you.
For I know that this moment,
This moment will not last forever.
For we will evaporate.

You will withdraw into yourself
    I will distance myself with my fears.
I will distance myself with my secret.
    Your fears will deny this moment,
You will gaze into my eyes, seeing my tears
    You will see my secret
Your fears
WILL MAKE ME BLEED.

T T T TESTOSTERONE

The first doctor that I saw
    For my hormone imbalance
Said that I needed some T T T
    T, Testosterone

Oh! I just cannot say that word!
    The first doctor that I saw
For my hormone imbalance
    Said some TTT, Testosterone would,
"Bring back my sex drive'
"Bring back my male aggression"

No! No! No!
No T, T,T, Testosterone

The second doctor that I saw
    For my hormone imbalance,
Asked if I would like to try Estrogen

"Estrogen hormone treatment" She said:
"Would balance me out"
"Might give me a sense of calmness."

Yes! Yes! Yes!
I would love to try some Estrogen.

T,T,T Testosterone, I cringe
When I hear the word
The thought of T T T Testosterones
    I cannot even say the word.

Estrogen, Estrogen
The word slips of the tip of my tongue
Hormonal balance is a good thing.

It is good when ones
        Body Parts and chemical make up match
I used to have a P P P penis.
I would devise different ways to hide it

Oh! How I used to hate saying P P Penis
        My body, my body
Body parts, body chemical make up.
It is good when they match

I have a Vagina now, Vagina
I do not try to hide that fact.
I have no shame over my body parts now.

VAGINA, VAGINA
        The word flows of the tip of my tongue,
Oh it is so good when,
Your body parts and chemical make up,
        Are all of the same gender.

SOME DAYS MIRRORS BECOME MY WINDOW TO MY PAST

This morning, when I gazed into my car's vanity mirror,
I saw John staring back at me.
That refection of my past is in front of me some days.
Some days, I look into the mirror, and I see John
John with his teary sad eyes looking back at me.
Some days the mirror becomes my widow to the past.
Last night I stood naked,
Naked, in front of a full-length mirror.
I saw a smiling naked woman looking back at me.
Last night I looked in amazement,
In amazement, I looked at me.
I saw my new body,
I saw my blossoming breasts,
I saw my somewhat shapely hips,
I saw my woman's crotch,
Last night, I was here, in the happy now.
Not lost in a lonely past.
Last night I gazed into a full-length mirror and I saw Janice.
Some nights when my make up has been washed away,
Some nights tiny gray facial hairs start to show,
Some nights the mirror becomes my window to the past.
Some nights, I see John in the mirror.
Some nights, I see those teary sad eyes looking back at me.

Mirror to my Past Picture

SHIFTING SANDS

Here I stand sipping beer again
Slipping away once again.

Standing on shifting sands, on the edge of Mother Earth,
Sipping beer once again.

Staring up into the consolations
Hearing the pounding of the rushing ocean.

Standing on the edge of shifting shores
Slipping away once again

The stars staring back at me
Mother Earth's shifting sands sliding between my toes

Here I stand sipping beer once again
Slipping away once again

All my senses;

All my fears, all my genders

All my sexuality

All my lack, of being a human being.

The pounding of the ocean, the shifting sand

The stars, all calling me home,

No dear spirits, I will stay here on mother Earth a while longer.

BACK UP LOVER

My passions often run hot
My desires sometimes get out of control
Dear back up lover,
Oh! How you please those secret passions and secret desires.
My passionless marriage to a husband incapable of pleasing my desires.
Dear back up lover
Oh! How I wish I could tear down these walls.
Dear back up lover Oh! How I wish I could
Escape this life that I live.
My passions,
My desires,
My wants, my needs.
Go untended to.
My husband, my children, my parents
Oh! How I tend to their needs.
Oh! Sweet back up lover
How I wish I were free to love you
Dear sweet back up lover.
Oh! How I need you. Dear back up lover,
Oh! How you tend to my needs, my passion, and my desires.
My prison is of my own making, years of fears. Fears of my true
    passions, fears of my true desires.
Oh! Dear back up lover,
You have taught me true passion.
You have chipped a way at my wall of fear.
Dear sweet back up lover
Oh! How I wish I could spend my nights in your arms.
Oh! How I wish I could escape this prison called a marriage.

SOME THINGS NEVER CHANGE

Whoa! It is 12:30 AM, Oct. 16, 2003 and the Boston Red Sox
    have lost another series to the New York Yankees!
Some things never change 1918 to 2003 is a lot of time with no change,
Change for me has been a constant state of being.
A constant flow of gender confusion and sexual orientation.
Baseball is just a silly game that I never could play; my father
    never took me to Fenway Park.
I always took my children to at least one baseball game a year.
It's not a gender thing it is a Boston thing, this rite of the fall season.
It is September/ October time for sport consistency,
The Boston Red Sox lose another playoff series to the New York Yankees.
My father never made an attempt to play baseball with me.
I miss playing baseball with my Jeanette, Oh! How she loved playing
    ball with me
Oh, how she loved going to Fenway Park.
Some things never change, my change just had to be.
1950 to 1997, my life was like a game.
I played the role of a man; I did all I could to win my father's
    respect, dare I say his love.
In my life there is this connection between baseball,
Fenway Park, my father and my kids.
It is all so silly; summer is turning into fall again.
I long ago stopped playing the role of male,
I remember the night my father died.
I was as tough as any of those Yankees and Red Sox players.
I played this role, with consistency, for my father,
As if my life was a sport.

The night before he died all he said to me was:
"Can you sneak me in a nip tomorrow?"
Consistency to the bitter end; dad, like the Yankees and the Red
    Sox, never did
Change; Dad never took me to Fenway Park.
It is so silly, another summer turning to fall,
The Red Sox again losing to the Yankees.
Baseball—just some how brings it all back
I wanted so much just for my father to hug me and say I love you.
He never did.

WHO ARE MY PEOPLE?

Who are my people?

As I wade through the rushing, incoming tide, I ask who are my people?

As I gather feathers for a dream catcher, I wonder.

Who are my people? Who are my people? The words roll through my very being.

This need to know seems to be coming to me from Father Sky.

Who are my people? I crave to know my ancestors. As I gaze into the wonders of the beach sky,

The sky is alive with the sea birds; the sky is a majestic rainbow.

The cloud formations, as a storm approaches, are full of messages.

As the strength of the rushing incoming tide almost knocks me over,

I feel a need to know my ancestors, who are my people? Who are my people?

Are the two spirited souls that I feel all about me, the ancestors of my people?

Are the spirits of the Seminole my people?

The Seminole people driven in to the everglades to die, chased to their death by US solders.

Chased to their death for accepting run away slaves into their tribe.

Who are my people? Who are my people? I wonder as darkness

Sets over the rushing tide. The rushing tides almost pulling me in!

Are the Algonquin tribes chased out of New England, into Canada by the US Army, my people? Who are my people? Who are my people?

I wonder in the darkness, I wonder as the rushing tides pull me into the waves.

My people, my people, my two spirited ancestors call to me.

Pulling me to the shore, pulling me to the shore.

Who are my people? Who are my people?

Are the ancestors of my father my people? The ancestors of those souls,

Those souls that crossed this ocean in search of life as the potatoes
    stopped growing.

Are these my people?

Who are my people? Who are my people?

I sit in the darkness of the night, I sit alone, yet not alone.

I hear, I feel, I sense, my two spirited ancestors all around me.

Are my people the ancestors of my grandmother's father, who
    crossed the ocean from France?

The sprit of my grandmother, who died the day I got home from Vietnam.

My grandmother, who spoke to me in many languages.

She was the only one who ever understood me.

Who are my people? Who are my people?

As I feel the softness of the sea bird feathers.

As I feel my self-flying in the ocean breeze, as I feel one with the
    sea birds.

I wonder. Who are my people?

My people yes my people the two spirited souls murdered by the
    invading Christians so many years ago.

My people yes my people. Rita, oh how she loved to dance,

Cause of death "Multiple stab wounds" Nov. 28th 1998.

Rita, oh Rita how she loved to dance. Nov 28, 1999

Arlington St. church, Boston Mass, the first Remembrance Day.

Who are my people? Who are my people?

Fredericka, Stephanie, Ukea, now Gwen.

My people yes my people. Nov. 20 this year,

This year we cry, we cry, once again

We do not moan, no, we do not moan.

We celebrate, yes we celebrate,

Who are my people? Who are my People?

My people are of two spirits, My people are with me.

We celebrate their lives, we do not moan, we do not moan.

This is a poem that has no ending for you see my people, my people

Live on, live on, my people are the two spirited souls that live on
    and on.

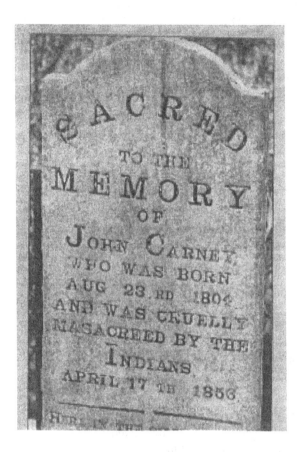

Was this a past life? A long lost ancestor? After all I was given the name John Carney at birth, handled down from my grandfather and his father. Way back in 1804, the Seminole Indians killed that John Carney not to far from were I live today. Was he just an innocent farmer or an Irish immigrant stealing the land from the Seminole people?

WAR AND PEACE
MAN AND WOMAN

A poem for Acts of Creation—
Woman Artists rising Speaks on War and Peace:

Man gave birth to warring nations.
Woman cried and screamed in the night
Over the death of their husbands and sons in far away lands,
Fighting other warring nations.
Men lead and boys follow off to war!
The male leaders with their screams of glory,
Proclaiming glorious victories!
Warring nations both claming "God is on our side!"
Male leaders of warring nations
Willing to send their sons of to die and to be maimed.
Male leaders of warring nations justifying their war.
This is about war and peace.
This is about man and woman.
This is not about gender?
No! It is not about male bashing!
How could I possibly be a male basher?
In my life, somewhat unique that it has been,
I have followed my male leaders off to war.
JFK, our President: "Ask not what your country can do for you but
     ask what you can do for your country."
JPC, my father and a proud WWII veteran: "The army will teach
     you to walk, talk and dress like a man. The army will make a
     real man out of you."

Two men that I put my trust in, my country's leader, my father,
    they sent me of to war at the tender age of nineteen, just months
    out of high school.
This is about war and peace, about man and woman.
This is not about unjust wars, or just wars!
This is not about Vietnam, WWII, and the Spanish American
    War, The Indian wars; it is beyond Iraq and America.
It is about warring nations.
This is about today; this is about our husbands, our sons, our daughters
Male leaders are failing us all.
Male leaders are destroying part of our souls.
Yes, that is what happens to souls that march off to war.
Part of my soul died in Vietnam!
Warring nations leave no winners only survivors.
Look into the eyes of a war veteran on Veterans Day or on Memorial
    Day! Stare into those eyes!
Stand back and watch a war veteran shake and cringe as the 4th of
    July fire works light up the night sky.
This is about war and peace.
This is about men and women.
My soul is forever scarred by our warring nation!
I never fired a shot in Vietnam. I preferred dying to taking another
    life.
Halfway though my year in Vietnam, I lost count of the dead
    bodies. I lost count of the horrid screams that I heard.
I sat in a bunker on a firebase that was on the edge of being declared
    over ran. On the edge of a direct B 52 drop.
I survived an ambush on High way One, an ambush that left me,
    beside the road, living among the dead!
I lived a score of years full of nightmares, drug and alcohol abuse.
Yes! 20 years.
"Four score and" the opening words from the Gettysburg address.
Was the Civil War a justified war? I declare NO!
Slavery was an excuse; the slaves could have been freed just out of
    common sense and dignity for all human beings.

No! A war between brothers, a war between fathers and sons, a war
over southern economy vs. a northern economy was not a just
war!
This is about war and peace.
This is about men and women.
So how can I end this essay, this rant, this alleged poem?
Our nation's men are at it again, once again leading us into a war.
Our husbands, our sons, our daughters are blindly following our
misguided male leaders.
I stand here today a proud transwoman.fighting for peace!
I stand here today as a catalyst for peace,
A link between men and women. Begging, pleading!
Men created war; it is time for women to create peace!

THE MIAMI BLUE

"What is it really except for a caterpillar showing off?"

What an interesting concept of a beautiful member of the family of butterflies. A beautiful member on the edge of extinction! What is a transsexual really except for a caterpillar showing off?

We transsexuals are the unwonted of the human species.

We live our lives as the caterpillars that we are born as.

We fight our very nature to weave our cocoons.

Our culture, our society, our very being fights our natural urges.

What becomes of those of us that do weave cocoons?

Oh! We are so much like the Miami Blue!

We also are on the edge of extinction!

When we burst out of our cocoons,

We are: Shot on the streets of Miami
> Trying to survive.
>
> Shot dead at our mailboxes in Jacksonville,
> for fighting for our civil rights,
> Shot dead, suicide by police in Tampa,
> Suicide by overdose in St. Petersburg.

So many of us on the edge of unemployment,
> On the edge of homelessness,
> On the edge of despair,
> On the edge of our personal extinctions.

Oh! We are so much like the Miami Blue.

Oh! I am so much like the Miami Blue.

I weaved my cocoon,

I flutter around in the Florida sun.

On the edge of extinction.

FRIDA KAHLO, AND I

Frida, Oh Frida,
It's all about facial hair.
To leave it alone,
To wax it, to pluck it,
To shave it!
Oh! Frida, how strong you where.
You left your eyebrows alone,
From eye to eye straight across your brow.
Oh! Frida, how strong you where.
You left your mustache alone,
Dark hairs,
Straight across your upper lip.
Facial hairs, should I leave them alone?
Or wax them, and pluck them,
Or shave them?
Oh! Frida! How strong you where,
You left those facial hairs alone.
Frida oh! Frida for my kind,
Facial hair is a cardinal sin.
To have laser treatment,
To have electrolysis,
is a must.
I fear rejection for having a Frida Brow,
I fear rejection for having a Frida stache,
Frida oh Frida, How I wish I had your self-confidence.
Frida oh Frida for sadly I wax, I pluck, I shave.

A TRANSGENDER PERSPECTIVE ON BISEXUALITY

My name is John Joseph I am a bisexual:

Back in 1999 I introduced my self as John Joseph, to the Bi network and the Boston Bisexual
Resource Center. Gender was not an issue. I had been seeking a group for support dealing with my sexual orientation as well as my gender confusion. Through their support groups and social activities I transitioned into Janice Josephine. Gender never was a question. I guess the question was: Am I a Bi-sexual man or a bi-sexual woman? This story is a dilemma for me! Yet I feel it belongs in this anthology, so here I go.

I have had sex with man from an early age, I learned from a family member that sexual favors could get you gifts. At a time in my life when I was positive that I was a female and every one in my life was telling me that I was a male; I found having sex with men made me feel feminine. Sexual orientation/ gender identity these lines often blurred in my youth.

My birth certificate at that time said male; it now is amended and says female. I am getting ahead of my self. Back when I had a penis if I had sex with a man I was called gay. In my mind at that time I was a woman with a penis thus I was having heterosexual sex. Now I know it was Bisexual, I think! From the seven grade on though graduating high school in 1969 I dated the same woman. She came out as a lesbian a few years after high school. Was I in a lesbian relationship all through high school? I survived three years in the army: A year In Vietnam and a year and a half in Germany. I explored both my gender expression and my sexual orientation

with man and woman during this time. I went way out on the edge as a transsexual sex worker in Boston for a year or so in my early twenties. In a wave of insanity I marred and lived the life of a middle class heterosexual cross-dresser in Southern New Hampshire
At the age of 45 the marriage ended, and my life begin. Here is where I will let the reader of this piece place a label on my sexuality. Yes at the age of 45 I was opening up to a Bi sexual support group as I seeked my true gender. Living in Boston during the first year of my transition. It seemed my gender struggle had reached its climax. I was rapidly wiping out any trace of my maleness. My last suicide attempt had pushed me down a road of sobriety and spiritual awakening. This separation of my 20 year life in NH, this rebirth into gender liberation had to lead some were! Here is when I wondered into the unknown. How does one separate gender identity from their sexual orientation?

When I first introduced my self to the Bi sexual community of Boston I was for most appearances a male. A somewhat, feminine male. I had sexual attractions to woman; as well as feminine transgender males. I went from John Joseph into Janice Josephine rather quickly. My gender was no longer in issue with me. I was female. What was my sexual orientation was the question? Even deeper then that; I was to learn that sexual preference can be as fluid as my gender was. So I presented this question to my Bi network group of friends, and I throw it out to all of you: Am I heterosexual, lesbian, gay, a bi male or a bi woman? I guess to debate this issue I have to be open about my sex life. So here I go. After my twenty-year monogamous relation ship with my wife came to an end, I found my self-back living as a woman. Through out that first year relied on emotional support from the many new friends I made at the Boston bi sexual resource center

In 2000 shortly before I legally changed my name and started my hormone treatment, I dated a straight male cross-dresser. For a few months he would come over to my apartment to dress up before we went out to a local club. Well the invertible happened we had a sexual encounter. Just seconds after he came, his body began to shake and he burst into tears. He was just repeating over and over again "I am not gay"," I am not gay!" I kept insuring him that I was a woman and that he was a man thus in theory; we did not commit a homosexual act. He did not see me for the woman that I was, he saw me as a man in a dress. My heart saw us as a heterosexual couple; his mind saw us as two gay men. The life of a transgender person is full of stabs in the heart!

Not long after this we took a trip to Boston together, as we walked the streets of Boston; he repeatedly walked a few feet behind me. Through out the afternoon he complained of a headache and asked me to stop being so "swishy" with my walk. We ended our relationship that night, he moved to Provincetown shortly after. He had told me many times that Provincetown was the only place were he felt safe dressed up. This is funny because Provincetown is the only place in Massachusetts where I feel uncomfortable. In P-town" transgender "equals drag show not much else! We will leap forward: It. At this time I am a post op trans woman; is 2001 I am in P-town for the premiere of my documentary "**TransJan**" at the Provincetown film festival. Walking down Commercial Street I heard an old voice from the past calling "Janice" "Janice", for obvious reasons. I am not using names here.

Once again I am charmed by a smile and the presence of this feminine man that I do so have an attraction too.

We do have a sexual encounter before the film festival is over. A commit is made seconds after he comes! in his eyes even with a fully functioning vagina, I still am just a man in a dress. Even after intercourse in his vision I am still a gay man. A heart carries many scars over the years So much for dating heterosexual cross-dressers. Time warp again back to 2000. I have been on estrogen hormone treatments and I have legally charged my name to Janice Josephine. I am now living back in Southern New Hampshire. I have developed small breasts, dropped down to a size 6 partite. I spend my Saturday nights in a club in Haverhill mass, dreaming of meeting the woman of my dreams. I have noticed for a few weeks a woman that is always alone and seems to be checking me out. My fears are that she like most people in the club are just playing the guessing game. Am I a man or a woman?

We finely dance, She now knows that I am a transsexual, the subject of my gentiles and sexual preference comes up. We end up dating and life is good for a while. The sex is great, even though I am incapable of having intercourse. The down side is that she is married; the thought of a jealous husband beating me to death hampers our relationship. Here again is the core of why I am writing this story for this anthology. This was my first lesbian relationship but was it? I had a penis, she had a vagina! She had a husband; I guess all in all this was my first encounter as a bi sexual woman. Then again I still had a penis maybe It was just me being a bi sexual male?

The fear of her husband beating me to death caused our brake up. Shortly after the breakup I met another woman that identified as a lesbian. Once again, I was in a confusing relationship. She moved in with me. Shortly after that she went from being supportive of my planned surgery into begging for me to stay the way I was. She still saw me as a man as long as I had a penis. She Loved being with a woman with a penis. I paid for the expense of her moving! She moved back in with her ex husband! She drove me crazy for a year with e-mails and phone messages begging me not to go through with my gender confirming surgery.

Oh I did leave out the one other sexual encounter that I had as a pre-op. My 50th birthday. I know this young trans man (I went to high school with his father!] He asked me what I was doing for my 50 th birthday, I had explained that since my family no longer what'd any thing to do with me, that I was just going to go home and cry a lot.

Well. We ended up buying some toys and exploring our new bodies how the testosterone had affected his body and how the estrogen had affected mine, made our bodies a wonderland of bisexuality. Still though I cannot keep from asking: He had a vagina and I had a penis so was it just another heterosexual encounter? I had my surgery and amended my birth certificate In Feb of 2002. After that sexual encounter at the film Festival I emerged my self in my writing and my activism I moved to Florida and started a new life. Last April I was doing a creative writing workshop, at the university of NH, in Durham. I met this delightful trans woman; something just did it for me. I did not find out into we were in bed if she had a vagina or a penis. You see it just did not matter; I love the female touch the female smile, a certain soft touch, regardless of what is under the skirt. I have learned that human sexuality is from the soul outwards.

The soul and spirit of John Joseph/ Janice Josephine is one and the same: Pre op, non-op, post op were stages of a life seeking inner peace. I thank all the wonderful friends that I met though the Boston Bi Sexual Resource Center; you all were off a great aid in my journey to bliss.

INTIMACY

OH intimacy!
I what it so much, yet I fear it so much
What is intimacy?
Intimacy is that special touch,
Intimacy is that special trust,
Intimacy is being part of some ones soul

Oh how I what intimacy yet how I fear intimacy.
The intimacy of trust,
The intimacy of touch,
That intimacy of sharing my deepest needs my deepest dreams.
Oh sweet intimacy, how I need, it how I fear it
Intimacy, in all of its forms. In all of its layers.

There is a special intimacy that we all place,
We place it in our doctors, friends, ministers, parents in our. Chosen
Loved one, in our siblings.

Oh! How I have been betrayed by all of them!.
Intimacy how I need it, how I chase it away.
Oh! How I need that special touch, OH! How I need that special trust.
Oh how I need that special person, yet how I chase it away.

Intimacy in all its forms, in all its layers,
I so want it, yet I so fear it.
I so want to be touched again, to be loved once again.
Why do I chase it away? Why do I need it so much?

I have found a doctor that I trust.
I have found a UU Minister that I trust
My Mother, half of my parents, has came back into my life,
My sister and a brother have returned my love; a fraction of my siblings.
My love of 25 years is gone forever!

Intimacy Oh! How I fear it yet how I need it
Intimacy, to be hugged once again,
Intimacy to be touched once again;
Intimacy, to be kissed with heated passion once again,
Will I ever have that again?

PRAY FOR THE
WORM CREATORS

Mean people suck, I know
It says so on the back of cars.
The meanest people of all are the worm creators
Mean people with so much going for them
Smart educated mean people
The worm creators.
Mean people that use their Goddess given talent,
To create pain and havoc
Pain and havoc on a massive amount of people
This is not a poem,
This is not a short story,
This is not a rant; this is more of a question.
What makes some people so mean?
What motivates someone to work so hard?
To work at creating these damaging worms?
May these troubled souls find peace and blissfulness.

I AM ON THE EDGE
OF OBLIVION FIGHTING
FOR MY SANITY

I am on the edge of oblivion fighting for my sanity; I just opened my mail.

The Disabled American Veterans Judicial Appeals office says: Sorry we do not help Transgendered Veterans. To quote them: "This office conducted a review of the materials pertaining to your appeal. Our conclusion is that your potential appeal does not present a substantial issue of fact or law appropriate for review by the United States Court of appeals for veterans claims under 38 U.S.C. SEC. 7261. We therefore are unable to defend you."

I am on the edge of oblivion fighting for my sanity! The leading advocate in America for Disabled Veterans agrees with the Veterans Administration policy of not giving transgendered veterans fair and equal medical treatment.

My next piece of mail was the: Gender Quest newsletter: "Rena Swift hawk Remembered" was the headline: Rena was a proud transgendered woman that also was awarded a silver star in Vietnam. I know her physical body died, but I was not aware it was from hepatitis C. I got a letter last year from the VA it said: "we are doing a study on Vietnam veterans due to the high level of Hepatitis C among them. Please come in for a free blood test." The letter was addressed to John Joseph.

I am on the edge of oblivion fighting for my sanity.

A note was just pushed under my door: Oh! It is from my landlord "Dear Landlord" is a great Bob Dylan song by the way!

Back to my letter it reads "I hereby require you to quit and deliver up to me on the 13th day September 2001 A.D. the possession of the following described premises, now occupied by you and belonging to me, situated in 25 linlew dr. apt. Derry NH. In said county to wit: cause: non payment of rent {RSA: 540:2[LL]{a]}"

I am on the edge of oblivion fighting for my sanity!!

"Dear landlord please do not take away my soul, dear landlord please do not put me out in the street, dear; land lord I know you have worked hard to get all your possessions, please take pity on my soul kind sir." Dear landlord actually fuck you asshole!! Am on the edge of oblivion fighting for my sanity!

I think a visit to Kindred Spirits Retreat will move me back from the edge.

A TRANS WOMANS VAGINA
MONOLOGUE

For V-day, and all the transgendered that have been violently abused. For my own child hood that never was due to incest, and painful penetration.

If your vagina got dressed, what would it wear?

My vagina would wear a sun hat, yes a sun hat, I want my vagina to be out in the sun, basking in all its glory!

If your vagina could talk. What would it say, in two words?

THANK YOU.

Yes my vagina would say thank you if it could talk; it would say thank you for the penile inversion surgery. It is hard for me to look back and reflect on all the pain I lived with, so I will not.

On Feb. 25, 01 I was awakened by the voice of Dr. Biber. I was in Mt.St. Rafael Hospital in Trinidad Co. It was my 51st birthday, and my first day with a vagina. On Feb. 24th I had a form of intersex surgery that constructed a vagina, were it should have been all my life.

Yes! I have a constructed vagina. Feb 25, 01, here I am a 51 year old woman with a one day old vagina. A puffy, sore vagina but my vagina!

Dr. Biber was checking out his work, and informed me that all went well, and that I was well packed to prevent it from closing up. I was still bleeding and in a lot of pain. Still, I could die in peace now. My body, soul, brain and spirit were whole at last. A court order declaring that I was a female was in the works!. Four days later, I was once again awaked By Dr. Bibers voice, and bright smile. The packing was coming out of my vagina. Today was the day I would see my vagina for the first time. I could not hold back my tears as the nurse handed me a mirror.

I placed it between my legs and sat up to look. I stared in amazement, My vagina was puffy and ugly! It was strange looking then again I never saw a vagina from this angle before Dr, Biber informed me that it would be a few months before all the swollen goes down. To day I had to start dilating, the dilating procedure was an important part of my postoperative care.

My vagina, yes my vagina would be oozing out blood and other fluids for the next few months. I would have to wear pads during this Period. At the age of 51, for the first time I had to wear pads.

Six months later, and all the swollen has gone away, and the need to were pads has gone Once again I use the mirror to take a look at my vagina. After, all these years of, self-loathing and feeling incomplete. I am afraid to look at my own vagina, my lips look too big! Still I hold then open with a mirror set up so I can see my vagina. I can see my vaginal orifice, I can see my urethral orifice my clitoris. I am crying again, you see I have a vagina; I am a whole complete woman. Dilating is no longer a medical chore, it now is joyful masturbation Feeling that vibrater deep in side me, finding that spot. That spot if I hit it right, my whole body vibrates in delight. That spot is my clitoris, my vagina. My vagina is part of me; I now can pee in a woman's rest room with out fear of being arrested!

Janice Josephine Carney
http://www.geocities.com/transjan1

APRIL 24, 2002, A WALK ALONG INDIAN SHORE BEACH

The beaches of the Gulf Coast close your eyes and listen
I have found the peace of the Gulf Coast.
Close your eyes and listen,
Can my words describe my bliss?
Can any words describe my peace of mind?
Close your eyes and listen
I took a walk along the beach last night
As far as my eyes carried me were incoming waves
As far as my ears carried me where the sounds, of sea birds.
My skin felt the warm ocean breeze.
My wondering mind was settled by the beauty of a gulf sunset
Close your eyes and listen
Can you see it, feel it, hear it, and sense it?
It is the peace of Mother Earth.
I watched the sunset slowly on the blue waters last night
I felt sand and water between my toes last night
I stared in to the eyes of the sea birds last night
So close to then on that thin line,
That thin line between ocean and sand.
Here is where Mother Earth and Father sky meet
The Sea birds fathered me
The Ocean waves mothered me
The setting sun eased my loneliness
Close your eyes and listen, can you hear it
It is the sound of this peaceful place I now call home.

SITTING ALL ALONE ON THE GULFPORT PIER

Under the full moon
In the quiet of the night
It is easy to be alone
Here under the full moon
The night wind whispering in my ears
The sounds of the waves whispering in my ears
Mother Earth and Father Sky are telling me
I am not alone
Under the full moon
I gaze at all that surrounds me
I am not alone
Surrounded by so many glowing buildings
Surrounded by so many people
I am not alone
Yet I feel so all alone
I saw smiling tonight

I heard music tonight
I took part in singing Happy Birthday tonight
Loneliness is a state of mind
Under the full moon
Alone on the Gulfport pier
Alone I guess but not really lonely
I shared my life tonight
I shared one of my poems tonight
Tonight I was part of someone's life tonight
I am part of the wind
I am part of the moon
I am part of the ocean
My state of mind is a state of bliss
Alone maybe but not lonely

A STATE OF CONFUSION

Wishing you happiness in your new apartment.
God bless you. God bless you.
Have a lot of happiness in your new life
Love, your Mom.
God Bless you, God loves you.
In your new life, in your new life.
My Goddess loves me, My Goddess loves me
She loves me the way I am
My Mother's God, the God of Pope Paul
Hates me the way I am
Pope Paul calls me "inherently evil;"
My Mother's God does not love me
My Mother's God does not bless me.
My new life
My new Body
Oh God! Oh Goddess! I know you do not make mistakes
Oh God! Oh Goddesses I am not a mistake, I know that
God loves me, God blesses me.
My Mother told me so.
My Mother loves me.
I chased my dream and I found my true gender.
My Mother loves me, my mothers God loves me
My Goddess loves me, My Goddess blesses me
The Pope is wrong. I am not "Inherently Evil"
Yes, I will find peace and happiness in my new life.
I love you too, Mom.

SLEEPLESS NIGHTS; YEARS AFTER THE WAR

Early in February of 1971 through early April of 1971, I lived and worked out of firebase Vandegrift along the Laos Border, northwest of the city of Hue. I spent sleepless nights through rocket attacks and a few ground attacks. I spent my days with a different assigned driver dodging land mines, ambushes and snipers along Highways Nine and One. I would spend my evening ensuring that all my line companies had their mail, and ensuring that I had all their out going mail for my next days mail run.

The last part of my day was spent on personal inventories, writing letters to someone's mom and dad. Forwarding mail to the hospital ship or to the hospital in Japan. My last duty before I tried to sleep was the **DECEASED** rubber stamp. Yes! I had an official return to sender **DECEASED** rubber stamp.

I was John Joseph Carney back then, doing all I could to convince myself of my manhood. It is August 16, 2002; I am Janice Josephine Carney today. I came to terms with reality six years ago and gave up on pretending to be a man. Last night I woke up to thunder and lightening. The Goddess's light show. Last night I woke up in the dark to the sound of incoming rockets, Last night I woke up to danger flares in the night sky. When I left Vietnam in 1971 I had a list of addresses of all those parents that I wrote to that I was going to visit, I was going to hug them, I was going to try to make some sense of it all. I never did; I burned the list one night hoping that it would help to stop the nightmares. I now know the nightmares are part of my landscape, part of John Joseph and Janice Josephine

There are two new sets of parents I have to add to that list, two more sets of parents that I wish that I could explain their deaths in an ambush, hug them and say there is a reason for all things. Did you know that we transgender people have our own wall? Just like the wall in Washington DC that honors Vietnam's lost souls. Yes, on the Internet *http://gender.org/remenber/people/ritahester.html*

I hugged Rita's Mother last Remembrance Day at the Arlington Street Church in Boston. Two new names Stephanie Thomas and Ukea Davis Back. AMBUSHED, in the night in Washington, DC just like in Vietnam, kids just finding out who they are ambushed in a hail of bullets just like Vietnam. Two innocent transgendered children sitting in their car, killed in an ambush. I have been watching the news stations, waiting to hear about the horrible murder in our nation's capitol, all there is is silence, Transgendered children do not count Black transgender children mean even less to the mass media

Having a conscious and a soul is a good thing, when it is alone and crying seeking answers that never come it is sad. I am alone full of tears, with no answers. I do not know what to say to Stephanie, and Ukea's parents.

THOUGHTS ON A CLEAR NIGHT AT THE WALL

[WRITTEN THE NIGHT OF MY FIRST TRIP TO THE WALL]

The night is hauntingly quiet, the sky bright, and alive. The bronze soldiers, one with a tear in his eye, come alive in the night. The grounds of grass, which they watch over, belong to the dead; as well as the living Veterans of the Vietnam War, in the loneliness of the night.

My anger still exists at the walls creator, as I look over a dark hole in the ground. As I inch closer and closer to the wall, keeping the memory of the lost souls of the Vietnam War alive. My knees start to shake.

A few inches of the ground the first lettered name appears on the black marble wall. It is the name of the last American Solder to die in Vietnam. The white lettered name stares back at me in the quiet of the night.

The reverse walk through Vietnam grows with the wall in the darkness of the night. The wall itself becomes alive in the warm night air. The black marble growing out of Mother Earth. The white names on black marble panel, after panel. Year after year after year. Name after name after name!

At the center of the wall two arches reach into the sky: The years 1959, 1975 look down at you the beginning and the end of the war. The war that still haunts my nights. In the clear stillness of the night I confront the black marble panels. The black marble panels reaching up into the night sky. The black marble panels, with there seemingly never ending list of names, from 1970-1971.

As I walk through the early years of the war, my main thought is: "It is best that I keep my emotions to myself." I reach the beginning of the wall, and I face the name of the first one of us to die in the war. At this point I redirect my anger,

I realize now that this memorial buried deep into the landscape of Washington soil, reaches deep into the soul of the creator of the wall. It is not an attempt to save the landscape of old Washington DC.

I see now what she visioned; the pain of the war lives on. Some how she has managed to see inside the souls of Vietnam Veterans.

My anger turns to question, why, why why,! Why did this wall have to be built? 1959 to 1975 was a long time. A lot of gutless presidents and legislators, my anger against them will never go away! I am somewhat glowing in the night. I know now that these names will live on never to be forgotten. A short dark path of America in a shadow of a wall that all Americans should walk.

Janice Josephine Carney, served in Vietnam July 1970 July 1971 as John Joseph Carney.

Vietnam, 1971
Firebase Vandergrift
Along the Laos border

Washington DC 2001

BOB HOPE JANE FONDA; HEROS OR VILLIONS?

FROM "*ONE HEART ONE MIND*" A VIETNAM MEMOIR BY JOHN JOESEPH CARNEY

The faces are aging, but every time I see Jane Fonda's Phony actress smile or Bob hope's standard grin, I cringe. The sound of their voices or the mere uttering of their names sends me back in time

Hanoi Jane was easy to hate without any explanation. How many American military personal died because Jane's visit to Hanoi convinced the leaders of North Vietnam that America had no willpower or the determination to fight very long to save the Republic of South Vietnam. Jane and her followers eventually convinced Nixon and Kissinger to give the Communist regime anything they wanted at the Paris peace talks.

The other familiar face, Mr. Hope, is a lot more complicated. How can any one hate Bob Hope? So many people ask me; after all he has done for American troops. The question I have asked myself over the years—did Mr. Hope do the U.S.O. tours to keep his career alive or out of the kindness of his heart?

I recall the day Bob Hope came to Camp Eagle in 1970. I was relaxing in front of my hooch, enjoying a little smoke, listening to Country Joe and the Fish, and reading "*Love Story*." I was just quietly daydreaming about being back in Cambridge, Massachusetts.

My moment of peace came to a sudden end when I heard the Executive Officer screaming at people that they had a top priority assignment for the next day.

It turned out that the high command was upset that Bob Hope could be embarrassed by a lack of interest in his current U.S.O. tour. To relate to this, you have to think about the situation. It was 1970; Bob Hope was a leftover from the song ad dance acts of the 1930's

When the U.S. Government saved his career by using him as a morale booster during World War Two.

See Bob tell a few old jokes, see him kiss the hottest new actresses direct from the big screen. See a parade of semi nude dancers, and then go back to the war in a better mood! After the "Good War," Mr. Hope made a string of second-rate movies, and then once again his shining star was in decline. Along came the Korean War and Bob Hope was back as the U.S. Government's main U.S.O. star. A special Christmas gift for all the troops in Korea. Bob was a star again. He had a huge network contract and new movie contracts. Throughout my early years, in the late 1950's and early 1960's, Bob Hope's smiling face in a wave of men and women in uniform was a common sight on network television.

By the middle sixties, the television specials full of the same old jokes and skits were declining in the ratings. Bob also was possibly making the worst movies of his career. Vietnam came along and, once again, a good old-fashioned war saved Mr. Hope's career. Once again, the U.S. Government supplied an all-expense paid trip to a war for Mr. Hope. More smiling, waving service men and women live from the war! The network renewed his contract. A huge Christmas Special loaded with smiles from Vietnam.

By 1970, there was not a soldier In Vietnam who had not seen Mr. Hope's specials from some war. We had all heard our fathers laugh at the old jokes and giggle as the dirty old man of comedy kissed some young new actress. Boston's old Howard was long gone, but Bob Hope was bring a new tits and ass show to network television. In fact, in 1970 Mr. Hope owned a good portion of the most valuable land in California and was one of the richest men in the country.

So there I was, as comfortable as you can get in Vietnam, when click, the Executive officer shut County Joe and the Fish off right in the middle of my favorite song, "*Fixing to Die Rag.*"

First he asked me how I could listen to that crap, and then he got on my nerves. As he was writing my name on his clipboard, he informed me that I was going to be a volunteer to see the Bob Hope show in the morning. There would be a formation at 0900 hours and I was to be there. The thought sent a chill down my spine—all those semi naked women dancers. Then the thought of Bob hope and those tired old jokes hit me. I declined the offer much to the dismay of the executive officer.

He screamed. "What, you do not want to see the Gold Diggers dance? What are you, a fag?" I refused to discuss my sex life with him. I just reminded him that the next day was Sunday and that I never miss service. He informed me that the Chaplin and his assistant were going to be at the show. I informed him that I was going to the chapel to pray unless he gave me a direct order to go to the Hope show.

I told him that I had seen the act already and that it was old and boring. He looked me in the eyes for what seemed to be forever then he put a line through my name. He called me a fag again muttered some thing about my Commie music, and then he went on his way.

Bob packed them in, a huge smiling crowed. They waved and shouted, "We love you Bob" They held up sighs that said, "there's hope with Hope." A perfect background foe another Bob Hope television special. More profits for Mr. Hope so he can buy up more of California. What can you do it was the only show in town. The U.S. Government was not going to fly in Country Joe and the Fish or the Doors.

The day of the show was the quietest and most pleasant day that I spent in the Republic of South Vietnam. The area was like a ghost town from the old west. Rows and rows of empty hooches, the medivac choppers sat silently on the helicopter pads. The aroma of good smoke filled the air, the taste of bourbon, and quiet conversation with a good friend.

Thanks Bob, for giving me this blissful day. Tomorrow, you will fly home to count your money as the rest of us go back to the war.

(Bob Hope went to his maker a conservative Republican that never saw a war that he did not like. He made millions of dollars from WW II, The Koran war and from the war in Vietnam. I saw Jane Fonda on CNN news show a few weeks ago. She said, "How dare any one call a Vietnam Veteran Unpatriotic?" On Memorial Day 2004 it still is an interesting question: Bob Hope, Jane Fonda Heroes or Villains? I still am not all that sure.)

A special thank you
to Chris Makary, for
trying to heal a wounded
heart and mind.

ODE TO THE LONELY

I HAVE TASTED ALL THE FLAVORS OF LONELINESS

Oh! How I remember the high School dances.
I was so lonely, no one wanted to dance with me.
I was a lonely adolescent transsexual in those days.
Oh, how I remember the single club scene,
All those lonely heterosexuals. I did not fit in.
I was a lonely heterosexual crossdresser back then.
Oh! How I remember the gay bars, I was so lonely back then.
Oh! How I remember all the lonely gay men, back then.
So many types of lonely people out there.
I have tasted them all.
Now I know the loneliness of the lesbian bars,
Oh how lonely I still am.
Heterosexual men, gay men, straight women, lesbians;
I have tasted all the flavors.
Still I am alone, you see.
I have solved my gender riddle.
You see I have found a measure of bliss.
Still my heart, my sex, my skin cries out.
Oh! This is just a short ode to loneliness.
Oh! Where is my kindred spirit?
Oh! Where is my soul mate?
I fear the wall of isolation that I have built around me
May never crumble.

REMEMBRANCE DAY
THOUGHTS

Nov. 28, 1998-Nov. 28, 2001

I am challenged to write. I am challenged to
Stimulate your minds, to stimulate your emotions!
Nov. 28, 1998-Nov. 28, 2001
On Nov. 28, 1998, Rita Hester was "brutally" stabbed to death.
How could it not be called "Brutal"?
How could her murdered have not been found?
How could her murderer not be forced to pay for taking Rita's life?
Why are we forced to walk the streets of Boston, knowing that
   Rita's killer could be walking behind us?
Nov. 20, 1995-Nov. 28, 2001
I am challenged to write, I am challenged to
Stimulate your minds, to simulate your emotions.
On Nov. 20 1995, Chanelle Picket was "brutally" beaten and
   strangled to death by one William Palmer.
How could it not be called "brutal?"
How could her murderer just be slapped on the wrist with a two-
   year sentence?
Why are we forced to walk the streets of Watertown,
Not knowing if Chanelle's killer is walking behind us?
Nov. 20, 1995-Nov. 28, 2001
I am challenged to write. I am challenged to
Stimulate your mind, to stimulate your emotions.
On June 16, 2001, F. C. Martinez was brutally bludgeoned to death!
How could it not be called "brutal"?
Killed by 18-year-old Shaun Murphy, just 18 years old and full of
   such hate!! How can these acts of hate happen over and over again?

Nov.28, 2001, I stand here today.

As a parent of a 21-year-old son named Shaun, as a parent of a 16-year-old daughter named Melissa, as a parent of a 14-year-old daughter named Jeanette.

I stand her today an out and proud transwoman; all I can do is live my life, all I can do is be an example of peace. Should some brutal act of violence end my earthly presence, so be it. I will not be forced to live my life in a closet! I will not be forced to live my life in a gender prison!

Blessed Be.

Janice Josephine Carney AKA Cedar Raven.

A 53 year old white trans-woman doing rap, may be a bit too much!

http://www.geocities.com/transjan1

A TRANSGENDER RAP

Hip Hop, Be Bop Rap on
Old beatnik prose,
Spoken word as a new art form.
    Two spirited, Low riding
      Gender queer Folk.
Is there a transgender beat?
A swaggering beat to being transgender
Is there a transgender rhythm?
A swaggering rhythm to being androgynous.
A hip hop, be bop beat of the gender variant,
A Hip hop, be bop beat to being gender free.
Hip Hop, Be Bop rap on
Old beatnik prose,
Spoken word as a new art form.
Two spirited, low riding
Gender queer folk
Queen Pen with her girlfriend rap,
Gay boys hiding behind
Their B-boys shields
Of gold chains and sagging pants.
Our beat is multi-racial,
Our beat is multi-sexual,
Our beat is multi-gender
Be bop, hip-hop be bop,
    Feel our heat
    Feel our fears
    Feel our needs
    Feel our pain.

Two spirited, low riding
Gender queer folk.
Be bop, feel our heat
Hip-hop, feel our pain.
Going stealth, Coming out
M to F, F to M; androgynous
Male, female, androgynous
Hiding for fear of our lives,
Hormones our sweet nectar of life,
Do not share that needle!
Do not spread that disease!
Hip-hop, Be bop Rap on.
Feel the heat that is our lives
Two spirited, low riding
Gender queer folk.
Flying under the radar;
Found guilty of gender-variant crimes,
Found guilty of bringing out so many fears,
Oh! How so many fear us!
Fears leading to tears, fears leading to tears.
Jobs lost.
Loves lost.
Families lost,
Homes lost,
Lives Lost.
Be Bop Hip hop, rap on.
Old beatnik prose
Spoken word as a new art form.
Is there such a thing as?
  Too Butch
  Too Fem
  Too gay
  Too lesbian
  Too straight
  Too Male
  Too Female

We gender variant folks, hiding
In fear of our lives.
Selling our bodies to survive.
Alcohol and drugs become our shields.
Drowning ourselves, in our seas of denial.
Spreading that disease,
That is, if we survive the next beating!
That is, if we survive the Mass Media's
Portrayal of us, as less then human.
Feel our heat
Feel our heat
A new freedom.
Transgender Liberation, feel our heat
Transgender Liberation spread our freedom.
Two spirited, low riding
Gender Variant folk.
My sisters, My brothers.
Be Bop, Hip Hop, Rap on
In old beatnik prose
In new spoken word art form.
My trans sisters, my trans brothers.
Transgender Liberation
Transgender liberation
Be bop, be bop
Hip-hop, hip Hop
Now is our time to shine, now is our time to dance.

MINISTERS OF HATE

The fundamental ministers all lined up,
One after another arrayed in a straight lines.
They shouted out their religion.
They stood in line waiting to shout it out.
They shouted out their biblical beliefs.
They were ministers from the Largo area. Ministers of hate.
Teaching their flocks pure hate
"We love you but we hate the sin," Their battle cry.
Ministers lined up to oppose a human rights ordinance.
They stood in line to use their religion, to control the city of largo,
Like their fellow Fundamentalists, who use the Qur'an to control
    women.
They lined up, one after another, using their Bible as a weapon to
    control,
They shouted out their beliefs.
Largo's fundamentalist and their flocks, using their religion as a weapon
Of ascendancy over
Largo's lesbian, gay and transgender citizens.
They shouted out misinterpreted versions of Leviticus,
Confusing shakhabh with shakav.Minister after minister, they
    shouted out to the city of Largo:
If you pass this Human Rights Ordinance, the world as we know
    it will end!
"God invented the marriage certificate."
"God said that only men and women could get one."
"If same sex marriage certificates became legal, all the heterosexual
    marriages will fall apart."
Minister after Minister of hate,

They lined up one after another, demanding that their religion rules
The city of Largo.
"The **normal** family will fall apart."
They tossed around the pedophile word.
Minister after minister they shouted out their biblical beliefs.
We cannot allow gay, lesbians and transgender human's equal rights,
  was their mantra.
The world as we know it will end!
Sadly, after the midnight hour,
Four out of seven of Largo's elected leaders agreed with them.
Still, three of the seven saw the hate and saw the need; they voted for
The human rights ordinance.
As for me, I left seeing more then ever why we need these so-called
Special rights.
After all some ministers of Largo churches have a special hate for
  me. More then ever I feel a need for anti discrimination
  protections under the law.

BEAUTIFUL NECCESSITES, PAINFUL NECCESSITES

"BEAUTIFUL NECESSITY" Is the title of Kay Turner's book on the art and meanings of women's alters. While in Guatemala, she asked a Maya woman "Why do you keep an alter at home?' The woman named, Virginia replied: "It is a beautiful necessity."
Beautiful necessities, beautiful necessities,
Painful necessities, painful necessities,
My life has been just that, a collage of
Beautiful necessities, and painful necessities.
Today I have a home alter, and it is a beautiful necessity.
Beautiful necessity, beautiful necessity,
How the two words float together.
The beautiful necessities, the painful necessities, of my life.
The beautiful and the painful where necessary for my bliss.
Beauty and pain are the seeds of a souls growth.
The pain of my childhood and adolescent.
The pain of my time spent in Vietnam.
The pain of a long lonely marriage.
All those pains where part of my beautiful necessity.
Beautiful necessities painful necessities.
My home alter sits on the landing to by loft,
Each night as I climb the stairs to my bedroom,
I stop on the landing to reflect on my beautiful necessity,
What a collection of gods, goddesses and special people and things,
Angels, two spirited shamans, my power animal, old pictures.

The painful necessities, a prom picture of John and Jean,
Over my alter are the pictures of a life time; John and a life time
Of gender confusion.
Yes all those painful necessities, were just the gateway
To the beautiful necessity that is my life today.
You see I know today that all those painful years in a mans body
Was just part of my souls growth,
I have grown into a beautiful woman out of necessity,
My home alter is indeed a beautiful necessity.

THE STATE OF NEW HAMPSHIRE STATES THAT YOU ARE A MAN

From my play: '*I WAS ALWAYS ME.*'

I JUST GOT BACK FROM A DISTURBING in Derry District Court, in my home state of New Hampshire. I was simply fighting a speeding ticket. I was clocked at 61 MPH in a 45 MPH zone.

So the town police officer pulls me over and asks for my driver's license and registration. He checks them both and then he asks me what my name is. I reply my name is Janice Josephine Carney. He then asks me if my name is Janice. I once again tell him my name is Janice Josephine Carney. He looks at me and then down at my license, then for a third time asks me what my name is! This time I respond with an attitude "YES" I am Janice Josephine Carney, Just like in the picture.

With a straight face, he then asks me if I am a man or a woman! Not "where's the fire." Or "what's your rush." Being somewhat startled by the question, I was slow to respond. He repeats the question, "Are you a man or a woman?" I cannot see any connection with that question to the matter of whether I speeding!

Controlling my strong urge to shout out "none of your fucking business" I politely say a little bit of each. By this time it dawns on me that the license has an M in the top right hand corner, and this police officer is fixated with that fact. By this time I am close to losing it. What does my gender have to do with it? Are there different speeding laws that apply only to woman? We have agreed that I am Janice Josephine Carney. This is my license and registration.

Shaking his head, he goes back to his cruiser to do a check on my driver's record. Now I am confident; I am a fifty-year-old driver with a perfect driving record. Yes, no record of ever receiving a speeding ticket. As he takes his time my mind wonders off. I am sitting alone on the side of a dark desolate road. Why is this police officer so concerned with what is between my legs? Why are my clothes a matter of question? Why does a driver's license even have to have our gender on it? Is his job speed control or gender control? Why does a police officer enforcing speeding regulations have to know what my birth assigned gender was? NH's finest at last returns with a speeding violation in his hand and the realization that he cannot arrest me for wearing a dress.

He gives me the highest speeding fine he can give me, in spite of my excellent driver's record. With a big smile, he feeds his ego, and says" have a nice night, sir!"

It is two months later and we both are in Derry District Court to relive that encounter. I get to ask the police officer some questions while he is under oath. My main argument is that if he had given me the benefit of a one-mile leeway on his radar gun, that my fine would have been half as much. This argument went nowhere. The police officer under oath stated that he had just checked his radar equipment and that it was 100% accurate. He also stated that he never gives anyone just a warning if they are speeding. He gives a violation. He then went on to say that radar equipment is always 100% accurate.

This, in my humble opinion opened the door for me to then ask why he felt he had to know my gender before deciding on a warning or a violation . . . I asked him if my lack of a gender had any impact on his decision to give me a speeding violation. As a few people in the courtroom had a good laugh, the judge informed me that I was out of line with my question. The so-called judge informed me that I could only ask the police officer questions directly relative to speeding regulations.

It seemed the police officer had the freedom to ask me anything he liked when we were all alone on a dark deserted road. Here in a well-lighted courtroom, I was not free to discuss what he said to me that night! Sensing that my point was never going to be reached, I at least hoped to reach a small measure of satisfaction.

I asked the judge what right does the police officer have to insult me in his courtroom. My name is Janice Josephine Carney, I am a hormonally balanced women. For all outwards appearances, I am a woman. I have the spirit and soul of a woman. I would hope you would stop the police officer from referring to me as "sir!" This got more uncontested giggles from the courtroom.

The judge informed me that in the state of NH I was a man! {I do not know what state law put him in charge of penis inspections!}

He then added that I had the right to wear women's attire, and that I had the right to choose how I wanted to be addressed. He said," Sir, how would you like to be addressed." Quoting a line from my favorite song [I AM NOT A F-__-__KING DRAG QUEEN] I responded with" Ms. Carney will do nicely!" The judge then informed the police officer to refer to me as Ms. Carney in his courtroom. I lost the gender war but I had a small victory.

I left the courtroom to stares and giggles, still very upset over the courtroom proceedings.

As I was paying my fine, I could hear the police officer joking with the court officers. I heard something about rubber gloves as I was leaving the building to their loud laughter.

Sitting alone, back in my apartment, I broke down into tears. I felt like having a strong stiff drink, a feeling I had not had in a long time.

Thank the Goddess that I now have the strength to control that urge. So here I am attempting to stop my bleeding heart! I had a sense of safety in this town that is gone now. If I am ever in need of police protection can that police officer stop laughing at me and come to my aid?

PEACEFUL

Peaceful is the emotion that flows,

The sun is setting in a big yellow glow.

Peaceful is the emotion that flows,

The silence is broken only by

The calming sounds of Mother Earth.

Peaceful is the emotion that flows.

Mother Earth's voices are chirping.

Her streams are flowing. Her streams are flowing.

Peaceful is the emotion that is flows.

Soon our circle of women will begin.

We will share our emotions.

Peaceful is the emotion that flows.

I hear a bee behind me,

I can see an ant crawling up the table beside me.

Spring is here.

MY DREAM QUEST

Do you believe in visions?

Do you have faith in the Native American tradition of a dream Quest?

A decade or so ago, I was living as a troubled middle-aged male. I embarked on a quest studying the old ways of the native North American Indians. I was seeking an answer to my inner loneness.

I studied from the course of the Good Medicine Society from Arkansas.

The Good medicine society is dedicated to keeping the old ways alive. After completing my courses and joining a Lodge, I was invited to meet a shaman and take part of a dream quest.

A member of our lodge had a homestead on land in the Adirondacks Mountains. I spent a weekend of meditation sweat lodge, and bonfires. It was living back in times before there were such things as electricity or plumbing.

On Saturday morning, I was invited to enter the T-Pee of the shaman. I was there to rest, to dream, to seek me.

As I closed my eyes and faded in to a peaceful state, a state of wonderful sounds and smalls. I saw my feet walking on sand in a long skirt. I found my self with painted toes and wearing a warp around skirt looking up at a blue cloud full sky. I say a paling reddish tree full of black birds.

A scene that I never saw in my native New England!

AT peace with my self and as I returned to the then and now, I was feeling a sense of renew. I described the dream to the shaman, she listened intensively, smiling and saying nothing.

When I entered a silent state, she called me Cedar Raven.

You are, cedar from the red tree, your power animal is a Raven, and you are Cedar Raven

She just smiled and said it is written, in my time I will find my inner peace. she went on to remind me that it was important for me to fallow my heart, and my true self would emerge.

A decade later, after cleansing my self of drugs, illegal, prescribed, and of alcohol and tobacco products, I returned to the good medicine society surprised to receive a letter from the same Crone that I had worked with in the past.

By this time I had charged my name and gender yet still was struggling with in inner loneness.

A year after retuning to my studies I felt a strong calling for many reasons to move to Fla. The land of the Seminole was calling, me.

The gulf beaches and the Seminole traditional lands were calling me home.

Not to long after settling into my new home, I walked out to my balcony to read and lay under the sun. Wearing a warp around skirt and noticing that my toenails needed some work, I set my ice tea down. I laid down looking up at the reddish pealing tree over looking my balcony. I listened initiatively to the flocks of black birds roosting in the tree. I gazed at the blue cloud filled skies.

A big black bird sat on my balcony reeling, singing to me,

I think he was welcoming me home. For, I was home at last.

DR. DAN KARASIC
DR. JACK DRESCHER

I am not a scientist or medical doctor. I am a transwoman. I do not have a lot of letters to put after my name just a simple BA in law studies from the University of Massachusetts.

The question of maintaining the DSM IV-TR is of major importance to me, though. As I see it all, this diagnoses did for me was save the insurance companies a lot of money. As long as the psychological professionals accept the current treatment of all gender questioning patients as having "mental disorders" those of us who are in need, of intersex surgery to match our genitals with our souls, minds, and body chemicals will be mistreated! We do not have a mental disorder!

This aspect alone is evidence in court that my insurance company should have reimbursed me for my intersex surgery, but the DSM IV TR and psychologist will, under sworn testimony, declare the insurance companies right. Where do the medical doctors stand on this issue?

Am I a mental patient who had cosmetic surgery that the insurance companies and the VA call {sex reassignment surgery, or gender reassignment surgery or gender alteration surgery]? NO! I am not!! I am a medical patient. I had a surgery [to quote DR. Biber] that was "antomically, physiologically and psychologically necessary for my own well being". I was a woman with a penis and Blue Cross Blue Shield was using the DSM IV to limit my medical expenses to six months of mental health. I do hope you can sense my outrage! In their view that my being a woman is a figment of my imagination according to DMS IV

I hope this letter will open the door for a hard look at the affect the DSM IV. Has on the medical treatment of all transsexuals. As editors of this upcoming issue [on gender identity disorders] in *The Journal of Psychology and human Sexuality:* Go beyond articles by "professionals". Please talk to and listen to people such as myself who have lived a transgendered life. Peace. Janice Josephine Carney
http://www.geocities.com/transjan1

IT'S TIME TO DITCH THE FIELD JACKET

Throughout the late seventies and early eighties, my whole life was focused on activism on veteran's issues. All my friends were Vietnam veterans; my whole life evolved around the Vietnam War. With drugs, (some prescribed, somenot) and alcohol I survived. I mean that as in, I did not live, I survived. My uniform of the day was jeans, a field jacket, and a baseball cap full of pins from various veterans' organizations. One day I stopped wearing the field jacket and baseball cap; my friendly VA therapist called it a major breakthrough. A few years later I was sober and drug-free. My true internal soul-searching had begun.

In 1997, with the help of that therapist {my Chris} and Dr. Shay I began my honest approach to my true gender.

I am at that crossroad once again. Once again, I have a wonderful therapist at the VA guiding me through rough life decisions. Once again I find my self surviving, not living. Once again I find my self as a full time activist. My field jacket is a name I call my self transgender, trans-woman. My whole life is dedicated to transgender issues. I am where I have to be most of the time. I seldom am where I want to be. Like the Vietnam Veteran with no personal identity or personal life, I have become a professional transgender person with no personal life.

This week I cried and cried; this struggle to simply live my last years as a woman doing what I like is over whelming me. When I discussed this with my current friendly VA therapist she compared it to taking off the field jacket. Maybe it is time for me to take off the trans label. Maybe it is time for me to separate from this safe comfort zone. It is with this deep thought that I resign as

Transgender Forge Director, and with good conscience step away from the role of transgender activist. As I close in on turning fifty-five, I am going to dedicate myself to my love of the arts. I hope to work on my writing and to be more active in Womens Artist Rising, as well as being more involved with building friendships with other women. Not the end, but a new beginning!

GOODBYE TRANS

Trans Jan
Trans Woman
Transgender
Transsexual
Transmission
The transmission on my old Saturn was broke
I had to fix the transmission or get a new car
Trans, this trans that
It is time for it all to go
I am Janice
          Josephine Carney
I am
Female not male
I once was male
Not female
I never called my self a transman
I never used the username transJohn
I never called myself a transgender
I never called myself a transsexual
I once was John
          Joseph Carney
TransJan
Trans-woman
Transgender
Transsexual
Was I a male?
Was I a female?
Am I a female?
Was I a male?

Am I neither a male nor a female?
Is Kate Bornstein right?
Am I a "Gender Outlaw?
In my mind Transgender:
Has become a way of saying that I am less then.
Transgender is a meaningless term
I am more complicated then a transmission
I never was broken
There never was a need to fix me
I never transitioned any thing!
I never transcended anything
Goodbye transJan
Goodbye trans-woman
Goodbye transgender
Goodbye transsexual
Like ditching the field jacket
It's time to drop another crutch and move on.

SOME FINIAL THOUGHTS

I AM BUT A VESSEL FOR THESE POEMS RANTS,
AND ESSAYS. The Goddess plants the seed in my soul
And I just pass them on.
For most of my life I looked at this birth
As a transgender/two spirited soul as a curse.
The Goddess has taught me that I was blessed not cursed.
To all my transgendered/two spirited sisters and brothers,
Live large, live proud for you also are blessed.
BLESSED BE: Janice Josephine Carney AKA Cedar Raven

A SPECIAL THANKS; FOR Ricki Liff;

I do not think my work would never have gotten edited and published with out the support that Ricki gave me in the last two years. Ricki and I have shared our struggles in overcoming our gender issues. In our own individual ways we have found our true genders. Ricki also has given tremendously to the whole LGBT community with her tireless work.

She is indeed a pioneer in the treatment of transgender clients by the mental health community.

Ricki has worked in the social services in one of the most conservative parts of America making her work that must more challenging and significant to the Transgender community.

A very special thank you to Marry Ross. Her editing job turned a mess into a coherent/ readable book.

Janice Josephine Carney

mailto:transjan1@yahoo.com

mailto:jjcarney@dav.net